International Basketry

Christoph Will

International Basketry

For Weavers and Collectors

Schiffer Publishing Ltd

Box E, Exton, Pennsylvania 19341

Translated into English by Dr. Edward Force

Originally published 1978 by Georg D. W. Callwey Publishers, Munich.
    CIP Short Title Acceptance by the German Library
Will, Christoph
Die Korbflechterei. Schönheit und Reichtum eines alten Handwerks
Munich, Callwey, 1978.

Printed in America.
ISBN: 0-88740-037-X

This book may be purchased from the publisher.
Please include $1.50 postage.
Try your bookstore first.

Contents

Introduction

Purpose of the Book

The realm of basket weaving is large. It includes all the countries of the earth and reaches back to the ancient days of mankind. The handicraft is many-faceted; the number of weavable plants, the raw material of weaving, is incalculable. The "types of wares", that is, the purposes for which woven work has been and is being created, can scarcely be listed. The multitude of creations of the weaving art gathered and preserved from ruin in ethnographic and local museums is little known.

The purpose of this book is to reveal all of these aspects and make them known to the people of our time, to demonstrate ancient techniques and portray working methods practiced today. This report is inclusive as a whole, but brief in individual details.

Only work with natural materials will be discussed, because these are appropriate to basket work.

Concept and Scope of the Word "Flechten" (weaving)

The word "flechten" with its derivatives and variants is, like the activity of basket weaving itself, age-old. It goes back to the Indogermanic stem, "plektan", from which the Latin "plectere" and the Greek "plekein" derived. The words "Flachs" (flax) and "Flaeche" (flat area) are related in meaning. The almost extinct profession of the Low German "Flaeken-Tuener", the flat rander, flat weaver, shows the root "plek" without the "t" of doing or making applied to the finished product. These "Flaeken" are matlike woven flat pieces that, in their airy and natural way, took the place of wooden boards, expensive in those days, in the construction of old Germanic houses.

The word "Tuenen"—randing, weaving—comes from 4 "Zaun", Low German "Taun", which we find in English 5 as "town", a city, a fenced-in locality. A garden too was 152–157 originally fenced in by dead or living willow rods which were woven. The walls of the early houses on the 147 European continent were woven, "wound" of fir branches 151 and hazel boughs. Thence came the name "Wand" (wall), as even the first edition of the Grimm Brothers' Dictionary proves. The weave was covered by straw clay; thus it included heat-holding open spaces.

The ancient profession of the basket weaver has remained alive. Particularly among primitive peoples, tribes not disturbed by industry, we find strong, graphic, creative talent that developed out of inner history. In industrialized countries too there are still inventive, highly

1. Woven, uncovered old panels of a barn wall, which became visible through collapse of the neighboring barn.

2. Opening in the panels of a woven barn wall, Lower Saxony, circa 1700.

82–84 trained masters working. A good basket, perhaps a hand-splint carrying or swinging basket, is still produced today in the ancient manner; the weaver prepares the splints by hand from the wood of the nearby or distant forest, builds them up and weaves them. Nobody knows how old the hazel workbench of the splint basket maker is, as an individual piece or an invention, for the basket maker himself often does not know which of his ancestors built it, seeking out the forked branch for the head that resembles a horse's.

It is also of no consequence whether the baskets made with such equipment are three days or three hundred years old. Both have the atmosphere of originality, even if the creative hand did not cut, smooth or use any part of them. These pieces will rarely reach an age of three hundred years anyway. Many old types of wares have disappeared completely due to technical advances of our time. 85 The fish baskets formerly woven by river fishermen 219–221 of willow, bark and all, have disappeared.

The Nature of Basket Weaving

60–72 At first glance it may seem strange when one says that woven work on objects for definite, enduring use cannot be done by machine, and that only even weaving strands of limited length, just as in textile weaving, can be made into yard goods on simple, only half mechanical looms. Out of the straightness of the willow the surface of the weave must be turned in one stroke to the form of the complete basket body. There the machine fails. Since the willow rod, the reed stem, the wood splint removed by hand, and the grasses have a limited length, even when weaving plants such as the rattan types often grow to a great length, they are not all suitablefor machine working. 60–71 This apparently disturbing limited length of the weaving materials essentially defines weaving: in the many millenia of basketmaking development one has learned to turn this mechanical disadvantage to a beneficial advantage.

The oldest handicraft of mankind has always remained in the shadows. But it has stayed alive. Even today a basket maker really still makes baskets, from beginning to end. Many basket makers still prepare their own willows. Thus they are, in weaving terms, still spinners, weavers, 60–65 cutters, dyers and decorators in one person and one process. The basket weaver prepares the willow garden, digs up the soil, plants it, tends the young plantation, harvests, stores, readies and works the willows, without needing a middleman. He always has his task of finishing his work defined by the nature of that which he weaves.

The building of a basket or any other woven work must form a unit from the beginning to the closing of the border. The concept of what is being built begins with the start of the bottom and must already include in its plan the border, 113–118 lid, handles or other components, the body, the bindings etc. To the basketmaker belongs the land he lives in, with all its customs and concepts. Let us think, for example, of the high valleys of the Stilf, west of Meran. There the slopes are steep; carrying the green wheat and mountain oats down to the village in carrying baskets, on one's back, is difficult. There the basket already has the shape and form for being borne on the farmer's back down the slopes to the valley when filled.

3. Messenger woman with wide, stout Saxon carrying basket. Woodcut by Ludwig Richter, circa 1850.

Let us turn to the fruitful plains of the Main and 229–231 Regnitz, the ancient river valleys around the old episcopal and imperial city of Bamberg. There the two east portals of the cathedral show a wealth of Romanesque archway decorations, facing each other, one after another. In the same manner, if a bit more modestly, the weaver applies his decorations to his carrying baskets in two, three or four rounds of varying types.

The Fichtelgebirge in eastern Franconia has its pointed 249 carrying baskets, that are called berry baskets there, because they are used for the gathering of wild berries. In their own way they are slim as the fir trees of these wooded hills, show a certain nobility of form, a restrained fineness that represents the ways of the quiet inhabitants of these old granite mountains. In the land of the upper Main, where the Frankenwald, the foothills of the Thueringerwald, and the Hassberge meet the Franconian Alb at a proper distance in front of the Rhoen, in which Lichtenfels and Staffelstein with its Staffelberg, the pilgrimage church of Vierzehnheiligen (Fourteen Saints), designed by Balthasar Neumann, and the Dientzenhof castle of Banz are located, the old Upper Franconian basket weaving art has developed, with its disciplined and yet richly decorated, pleasantly formed and strongly original basket weaving work.

Characteristics and Advantages of Woven Work

The always progressive development of the natural sciences and technology have, as mentioned, scarcely touched the weaving art; ancient, quiet and untroubled it stands amid the swirl of progress. Yet it has not thereby ossified; again and again it has known how to find new ways. It remains slow, careful, tedious in terms of working, This slowness in workshop procedure has nevertheless prevented it from giving up its healthy original stability and methodology too quickly, and so processes, concepts, forms and goals have been maintained for hundreds, even thousands of years, to the present day.

The clear, precise construction of woven work gives joy. The process of its formation is there for the careful observer to see. Natural weaving materials and handwork are today, as in olden times, the objects of many people's secret longing.

Good-quality woven wares therefore were and still are maintained like friends, passed on from parents to children and handled lovingly, protectively. Even the simplest weave is an ornament, readily recognizable to the eye. The transition from purely useful weaving to color and decoration crosses a line so fine as to be indistinguishable. That makes every kind of weaving, all the details of an entire woven object, so rich and full of life.

The miracle of firmness along with such lightness is achieved by the nature of the woven materials, which win flexibility and toughness in their struggle for life. The willows, hazel rods, wood splints, reeds and birches, the rushes and bamboo from overseas are all light and yet firm, tough and full of tensile strength. Almost all weaving plants are "fighting plants", they must endure poor or rich soil, long dry spells and periodic rain and flood, heat and cold. Some grow strong in poor limestone mountain soil and provide steel-tough rods. The salt-water rushes that stand in turbulent seas are tougher than the pond reeds that grow more tranquilly.

The nature of randing, winding weaving achieves, along with restrained flexibility, the inimitable firmness and carrying capacity of the basket. The weaving plants, whether left in their full natural roundness or split according to their natural fibers,have a very high resistance to tearing, of which tension, elasticity, is as much a part as great flexibility.This is not granted without the resistance

of the raw plant, which wants to grow straight and must stand upright. Thus there is often a certain hardness of the outer surface, above all that of the fibrous rodlike weaving plants such as the willow, the foreign rattan and others. It is in and of itself resistant to pressure. This resistance is even increased through the weave's limited but sufficient ability to give way.

4. *Randing and fitching weaves. Above: Origin of friction through the effect of the weave, that is, the pressure of the bent willows. Seen from above. Center: Old Cretan ornament (wall painting) in strict circular geometry. Below: Upper closing of a fence, fitched. Branches broken from a tree are set in.*

This "give", that certain softness of the weave, can, like its firmness, be determined thoroughly as to its degree by the basket weaver. The choice of material, that is, the nature and choice of the individual rods, the hardness of their outer layers, the tension, the distance between stakes, which increase firmness as they come closer together, the closer proximity into which the weavers are beaten, all are important in determining the stiffness or flexibility of a basket. Thereby the mass and strength of the rods, straws or fibers play a decisive role.

If a basket, whether large or small, whether woven of the finest, almost tissue-paper-thin strands or of whole rods and fibers, falls to the floor, it will neither suffer nor cause damage. It is the aforementioned flexibility, the weave loose enough to absorb pressure, the bendability of the willow weavers, that causes this unbreakability. The basket with its windings causes in its fall an air pressure that breaks the fall, making the impact softer. But this unbreakability also has its limits; if the weaving wood becomes too old for its conditions, it becomes brittle and breaks more easily than when fresh. Lack of care and cleanliness increase and speed up the decline, as wind and weather drain the lye from old wood, warm damp storage brings on worms and fungus as destroyers, especially when the wood is felled at the wrong time. Above and beyond their unbreakability, woven wares, when well-made of healthy wood, endure remarkably. A laundry basket, for example, with woven bottom, sharmed willow corner pieces, holds up well through two generations when handled with care. Thus there are hand baskets, well cared for and protected, preserved in museums though wellnigh two hundred years old.

207 The woven laundry basket with likewise woven ventilated bottom, particularly when fitted with a cover of muslin or the like, blocks the view into the basket, yet lets the inside breathe and thus hinders the growth of mildew. The airiness and ventilation can be seen particularly in 132–145 construction weaving, especially in coverings that, in the large halls of smoky public houses, are meant to disguise an ugly or functional ceiling or roof construction. The light weave blocks the upward view, but lets the smoke and hot, used air escape.

A dividing wall on a balcony, made of light, open weaving, blocks the view in, but allows the person sitting near it to observe his surroundings without being seen himself. One might call it the "curtain effect".

One should also look at woven work in the different lights of day and evening, and take the time to observe the play of light and shadow on the weave. The shadow thrown by a basket or a lampshade, for example, with a broken weave, offers a completely new appearance.

287 Consider the wide wooden splints that are woven in many ways. With light to the front or back, through the variety of crossings in the manifold forms of a six- or eight-cornered weave, according to the number of splints that cross each other, a wealth of shadowing in numerous degrees of lightness will result, geometrical decorative forms will show themselves, such as one can see in Moorish ornaments in North Africa or Spain. Then even a modest weave becomes rich, as if enchanted. Weaves can

be made completely opaque, just as one can also make them watertight. Very thin, translucent materials or very open, spaced weaves and patterns afford lightness. Lamps can be woven so that the bright direct light strikes only the floor, the table, or the ceiling or a wall of the room. The shade can cut off too much upward light. But a light weave, according to the form of the shade, its height and situation, affords rich effects of light and shadow play.

Fine weaving splints, such as esparto splints or the thinnest willow skeins, give a mild light, restful to the eyes, as did windows of thin animal hides in olden days. To be sure, there are weavable glassy artificial stuffs nowadays, such as polyethylene, which let dull or even clear light through, and they are very useful as construction weavers in smoky rooms, as long as they keep out heat or cold. But because of their greater weight, except for Saleen, the lighter plant materials generally have the advantage Weaves can scarcely cut off, limit or dampen sound by themselves. They are not thick or heavy enough to do so. But rushes, reeds and straw rolls can be used by capable basket weavers and inventive architects to deaden sound. At the same time they are also decorative and, by their structure, an excellent shaping material. Sometimes the individual surfaces or plates run flat and even to ceiling or wall, or diagonally or even at right angles, but there is also the possibility of using the weaves themselves, very roughly in terms of material and very three-dimensional in weave, by using the so-called Dueten weaves or other types. The uneven areas that appear then become at the 136 same time decorations, rhythmical structures of a special, unusual type.

Wood keeps you warm, as everyone knows. The woven woods are particularly warming, because they include countless air chambers. Air is a poor conductor of heat when it is enclosed in small cells and cannot move. Thus the willow, with its soft, not very thick, air-holding wood, keeps heat in and turns coldness away. .

Willow weaves also do not let in dirt and dust very easily. The smooth, waxy growth layer of the peeled withe catches as little dust as the glassy-skinned natural tube of the climbing palm of Indonesia. The same is true of the fine, non-greasy smooth sheen of the hand-cut pine splint. 69–71 Rattan (calamus), freed of its glassy layer of skin, is somewhat rougher. It needs a covering of varnish, lacquer or wax, so that dust cannot penetrate into the open pores and fine rough spots of the silicic acid crystals. Dust, as well as dirt, bits of food and oil etc., can nevertheless work into the cleanest weave. Then one must brush it out or wipe it with warm water, or if need be with soapsuds or a mild dirt or fat remover, or hold it under running water, to get it clean again. Dust can also be removed very well from dry woven objects with a vacuum cleaner. This is particularly true of bath mats.

The willow as a weaving material is also a poor conductor of heat. Therefore a firm mat of peeled whole willow rods and stakes holds the warmth of bare feet much better than any other floor covering during intense cold. In baby play pens it warms and exercises the feet, makes them firm.

The question of when willows should be cut so as not to be attacked by worms or fungus is similar to that of when ordinary building wood should be cut so as not to burn.

The healing power of the weaving plants, indeed of weaving activity in general, the magic powers of soil types and forest areas in which good trees for providing splints are found, the footpaths and ponds along which reeds, rushes and cattails grow, the remarkable qualities of the willows, the whole realm of botanical lore to which the uniqueness of weavable plants is related, all of that permeates this handicraft and those who work at it, whether they make single pieces or whole series. Nothing about weaving plants is poisonous, neither in the growing, picking, preparation nor use of them, particularly when one uses unfertilized or naturally fertilized plants. Natural powers and juices are present to share their health with man. (In the lore of natural healing, for example, a medicine for weakness of the stomach is made from three types of willow.) For the buyer and user of woven goods they are harmless, above all when produced without coatings of nitrous lacquers.

As the aforementioned laundry baskets are airy and dry, so herders' pouches and similar products of wood splint work and straw roll technique are good for holding freshness and moisture. Thus, for example, a flat plate of straw roll weave, bound with pine splints, will keep a shepherd's pie of pastry or raised dough in a moist, warm, tender condition, unlike porcelain, metal, plastic or hardwood plates; the straw sucks up the moisture eagerly, so that it does not become mushy. The empty plate can then be cleaned under running water and air-dried in the shade.

Mysteries and Peculiarities of Basket Weaving

It would be remarkable if a handicraft that reaches from dark prehistory did not have its mysteries. Thus the "basket curve" and "basket arch" have made their way into geometry and thereby into architecture. To the realm of the magician, the illusionist, for example, belongs the so-called "peasant finger", a woven tube about as long as a pencil, of thinly cut, usually colored palm leaf. It is made in much the same way as a hose weave, the socalled plaiting weave or braid in the realm of mechanical weaving. If one slips the colorful peasant-finger tube over a finger and then pulls on it, it is at first impossible to remove. The finger can be torn off more readily than the tube can be pulled off. The secret lies in the fact that the diagonally randed twill weave of the smooth and thin straws becomes stiffer and thus narrower when one pulls on it. Only when one pushes the peasant finger back, presses it together, thus doing just the opposite of what one would do to draw the tube from the finger, does it loosen, because it becomes greater in circumference again and no longer encloses the finger so tightly.

Like many other occupations, weaving also knows the knot, in loose and open as well as more tightly tied form. The knot in its simplest form is related to the pretzel, and has a lot to do with the mechanical weaving process of crossing (knots plaited over stakes and weavers).

Characteristics of the splint-providing conifers, for example, can be judged much as in violin making. When the wood isfloated to the valleys from the high mountains in spring (rafting), one recognizes the best logs because they sing. These are sought out by the violin maker as well as the splint basket maker. For both artisans they are the ideal working material, that gives the best results.

Obtaining hand-removed splints calls for a lot more work than making knife-cut or machine-cut veneer strips. The hand splint is then tough and tense, while the machine splint, cut with the machine's brutality over wood and flesh, splinters and often breaks. Even the oldtime carpenters said that beams cut with the broadaxe hold considerably better than those cut by saw and worked by machine.

Good weaving work thus requires corresponding work time. The preparation of the willow strands, like the removal of splints by hand, costs much effort. And where can one still get good straw? The fact that, on the other hand, few tools and for the most part only one man are needed to finish the job equalizes in part the expenditure of work.

HISTORY OF BASKET WEAVING

Pre- and Early History of Basketry

Regarding basket weaving as an ancient handicraft, perhaps the oldest craft of mankind, is based on the fact that for it, aside from the human hand with its fingernails, neither tools nor fire were used. Many of the materials, such as reeds, can be picked with the nails, others can be broken off, such as evergreen boughs for building shelters. But it is precisely this simplicity of work that is the reason why no concrete evidence for prehistoric or early historic basket weaving is at hand. Fire destroyed the dry, easily inflammable woven objects, and what was entrusted to the earth rotted.

5. Madonna with thick fence. Uppermost strokes fitched. Copperplate by Martin Schongauer, circa 1470.

The actual age of the first basket weaving can therefore not be determined. All that is clear from the history of the European peoples is that here basket weaving was a family, farm and household business, one activity among many, and that it developed, late enough, into a sideline occupation alongside the farmer's work or a primary occupation in times of little farm work for small farmers.

One can argue about whether basket weaving or construction weaving came first. That brings up the question of when the basket and the fence originated, of the origin of actual baskets and plaited fences, including house walls. No fences or bulwarks have been dug out of the rubble of the millenia. They stood above the ground and all too easily provided firewood, or they rotted completely away, leaving only a bit of black earth behind. But a few remains show clearly that building houses through the use of woven walls (and woven roofs) spread with clay mixed with straw, warming and warmth-holding, was practiced very early by the peoples in our latitudes.

Fortunately, fired pottery has built a bridge here. Baskets, woven containers, were covered with clay or fine loam and fired. The weave charred and disappeared. But its impression was retained in the hard-baked clay, giving a picture of simple space-forming weaving. Engraved decorations that clearly portray weaving or the effect of weaving are often found on shards.

From the old Chinese culture too, with its outstanding achievements in many areas, evidence will presumably be provided within a reasonable time that will allow us to examine the origin and development of the weaving art there. At this time Egypt, with its Cairo Museum, is the most productive source of woven work preserved from ancient times and comparable with present-day work. Egypt already had a highly developed weaving culture about 3000 B.C.; it had obviously developed long before. The comparatively germ-free and very dry air in the stone tombs, and even in the buildings around them, hindered the rise of destructive microorganisms, so that along with other cultural objects, woven wares too remained well preserved.

In addition, the Trade School in Lichtenfels possesses several Indian pieces, which like the Egyptian were in rock tombs and which go back to pre-Columbian times. In these too there are similarities in workmanship.

Whoever has the time to compare North African woven work of our time with those pre-Christian museum pieces will find to his surprise how little has changed in technique and formative execution. The basic art of weaving was an ancient art, and the principles of all weaving operations always followed the laws of nature.

In the same way the small and large reed boats of the Indians on Lake Titicaca in South America are evidence of technique maintained over thousands of years.

6. *Old Egyptian clay container, imitating a weave, circa 2000 B.C.*

In the German-speaking area, along the Bodensee baskets have been found that belong to the later Stone Age or the Bronze Age. In pattern, construction, material, binding and weaving they are very similar to the large struck weaving of today, that is, baskets of barked or white-peeled whole willow. In this area, a crude one to be sure, scarcely anything new or better has been invented since then. There we have actual works of genius with opened-out bottoms, with foot borders formed of thick upsetts, with the horizontal layers in a special linen-binding type of weaving, and the border as a deliberately knotted rim formation.

104
105

Also, the battle shields of the Teutons, covered with buffalo hide, were woven of willow. The swinging weave

7. *Process of making sling rounds, with variation of stroke length and direction, and fitches turned from skeins.*

8. *Firmly and lightly drawn-out rounds over horizontal and vertical stakes.*

9. *Slewed weave with zigzag multiple twills, of willow skeins.*

hindered the sword blade's penetration, since it did not find enough resistance. Such shields were woven in our times for Wagner's "Twilight of the Gods" at the Bayreuth Festivals at the express wish of Wieland Wagner. In addition, the police of various countries use woven shields today to ward off sticks and stones.

The evidence of Langobardic woven ornaments, mostly carved in stone, portrays multiple fitching. These fluid images of woven weaves (without the stakes) make an unusually strong impression. The Celtic-Romanic ornamentation too, like the early Germanic, often shows weaving processes of high quality. If they lack the strictly geometric ornamentation of the Greeks, still they express a strong free spirit.

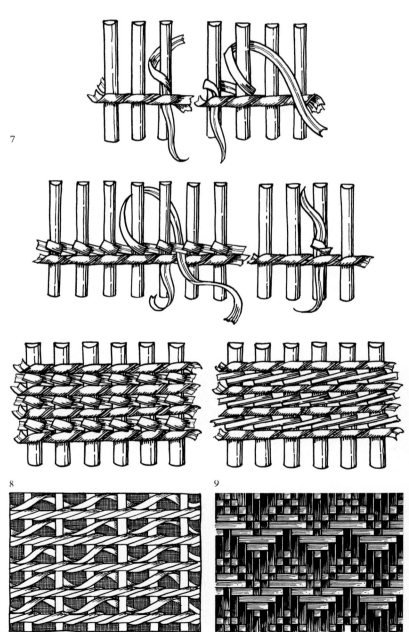

7

8   9

10. Vaulted cellar with weaving basket makers working together on a willow field marshal's figure (monument), from the Encyclopedia of Diderot-d'Alambert, copperplate, circa 1770.

The old Celts, as Caesar reported, wove more than life-size figures of gods out of willow. Even at the end of the Eighteenth Century a cellar view in the Encyclopedia of Diderot-d'Alambert shows basket weavers plaiting a Roman monument figure. Willow planes and adjustable

11. Roman society lady surrounded by servants doing her hair. Bas-relief stonework found near Cologne, circa A.D. 200. Clear portrayal of the willow chair frame, with square and layered weaves.

12. Three-dimensional armchair with seat cushion, carved in stone. Recognizable wide splint and fine full willow work. From a Roman grave.

thinners shown by Diderot are also significant. In the National Museum in Naples marble sculptures are found which show full-sized baskets with their decorations as extraneous work. Their similarity to the full willow baskets still made in Greece today is unmistakable. But the artistically experienced Greek people must have achieved more in basketry before the Turkish invasion than can be seen today. The mysteries of Grecian knots testify to this. In the Roman-Germanic Central Museum in Mainz too there are excellent, splendidly preserved carved stone works from Roman times with portrayals of woven basket furniture, among them a three-dimensional basket chair, a stone representation in a grave vault from about A.D. 200. A small basket with a lid, presumably woven of willow strands, with metal and leather decorations and a wooden bottom, shows what one knew how to weave then. We also find in Crete an ornamental band which portrays the external view of a fitch, a wound staked weave in strictly geometrical form. The more than merely utilitarian significance of the antique weaving art is shown there and at other Mediterranean locations in the Meander and the Running Dog patterns that spread over the whole world, with symbolically strong weaving in many repetitions and variations. All these evidences in works of art, paintings, hand drawings, woodcarvings, engravings and lithographs, in the works of wood and stone carvers, are much clearer, and reach farther back, than the real objects. There are numerous portrayals of the weaving art, such as an old Roman mosaic in which a basket full of flowers is shown. Remarkably, the formation of this kind of weave has remained the same from that time on. The Basket Museum possesses a woodcarved, gilded basket from the Baroque era with the same type of weaving. But it must, according to all attempts to duplicate it, represent reed or rush work which, unlike willow work, can be pressed very closely together.

Still in all, we cannot set exact time limits for ancient, antique and medieval weaving, nor for the beginning of modern weaving. Though again and again new weaving materials appear that allow and encourage new weaving types and effects, on the other hand it is perfectly clear that since the Bronze Age, if not significantly earlier, certain basket weaves and styles were and are used over and over without diminishing their effect. Unfortunately, though, there are no remaining objects, documents or reports of how long, for example, the back-carried baskets of the Franconian, Bavarian or Hessian-Thuringian settlement areas have been common, and how far they have developed out of the simplest foreign forms, or if they emerged complete. Willow furniture resembling beach chairs can be found in copperplates from the Netherlands, from the Seventeenth and Eighteenth Centuries.

The Bavarian National Museum in Munich possesses a finely worked original basket from Florence, made around 1500. The doll rooms of the Germanic National Museum in Nuremberg show many lovingly created miniature woven works, attributed to the Baroque or even earlier eras, mostly made of the thinnest willow tops. The Toy Museum in Nuremberg also possesses several beautiful pieces in its doll rooms and a shop for basket wares.

⁴⁰⁷

But no discovery, no depiction leads us back to the gravestones of the late Roman times. The making of bowls, whose existence and origins we can trace back to the Chaldeans (about 6000 years) most definitively and, thus far, most directly thanks to the cleric Jurgen, who himself came out of the bowlmaking trade, extends into our own times, though it is, to be sure, dying out.

¹⁶²

The Profession of Basket Weaving

This old handicraft was made into a well-organized occupation very late. Although in the beginning it had preceded all others, it happened that, with the increasing sophistication of the types of work in all handicrafts, it was the last to receive its constitution as an artisans' guild. In 1593 the first basket makers' guild was founded in Braunschweig; the Munich guild arose at about the same time, to be joined quickly by other localities where lodges and unions had been formed centuries before.

Long before the founding of the basket makers' guilds, the newly flourishing cities were supplied from the country, the farms, until as the cities' population grew, the basket makers moved into them in steadily growing numbers. But that did not cause deliveries from the nearer and farther villages around them to stop. In documents it is often noted that the "City Basket Makers" complained about the flooding of the markets by "Stoerer" foreign to the cities. "Stoerer" were originally basket weavers or other artisans who "went to their work", worked for city dwellers or the larger farmers, making baskets or other objects for a salary. In the process these basket makers either brought their own willows with them, or their employers had supplies of them. So these workers not only took business away from the city basket makers, but also lowered wages.

In the process of gaining occupational freedom, the guilds grew into unions, which later acted as forced unions, which every artisan had to join. The unions' pressure was, however, lifted again, mainly after the two

World Wars. What is remarkable is that the basket makers' guild in the upper Main Valley around Lichtenfels, Michelau, Marktzeuln and Burgkunstadt arose only around the middle of the Eighteenth Century.

In these times the willow creations from Michelau, Burgkunstadt etc., were carried, sold and transported on barrows into the nearer and farther surrounding area, finally into foreign lands. The tradespeople, who had to change the winter and summer activity of the Upper Franconian basket weavers into jingling coin, were called "Basket Pushers". At first only barked willows were used in modest forms. Later one began to peel the willows white and achieve finer work.

In 1773 a small basket made of split, planed and slimmed willows was displayed, made by the Michelau basket maker Johann Puppert. The clues to the events of this not too far distant time have disappeared. Reality, presumption and legend can no longer be untangled from each other. The story goes that a wandering journeyman from nearby Thuringia, out of gratitude for his hospitality, showed the alert and talented Johann Puppert how to split, plane and slim willows into skeins and work them into baskets.

¹⁹⁴

^{73–76}

This way of preparing full willows must already have been known to the ancient Romans. For it one need only turn the willows, that is, drill into them along their long axis, as is done with laundry basket handles, and they split lengthwise. Thus the splitting process is grounded in the nature of the willows. The author has had the good fortune of becoming familiar with the preparation of hazel skeins in the basketmaking village of Schoenau vor dem Walde, near Gera in Thuringia, and at the same time to see hazel skein work in the same simple form as that of the first basket made by Puppert (a treasured masterpiece at the Trade School in Lichtenfels). Only through Puppert and his at once highly talented, hardworking and joyfully inventive Michelau neighbors did the originally simple full willow work turn into a superlative art, such as one finds with other weaving materials and plants in Japan and China, Thailand, Indonesia, Mexico or Central Africa.

¹⁹⁴

^{384–388}

In the process of developing fine-quality weaving among Upper Franconian basket makers, the new products were sent farther and farther into the world by the basket dealers of Lichtenfels, Michelau and the region. They went as far as Egypt and the United States. The basket dealer Aumueller of Michelau even experienced a shipwreck, from which he saved himself by swimming ashore. In these trips the basket dealer, who knew basket making, learned new things everywhere.

Since the end of the Eighteenth Century, Upper Franconia had led the way in German basket making,

15

13. *Delivery from the basket-making villages to Lichtenfels.Light ox-drawn flatbed wagon; large shipping crates of pine hand splints for the basket industry, made in Mistelfeld, circa 1906.*

14. *Basket maker with clothes hampers ("wash-puffs"), with the carrying rod over his shoulders.*

15. *Basket maker woman carrying her baskets packed in a delivery bag on a "Troung" carrier. The bag is to protect the "new models" from too-early imitation.*

16. *Deliveryman with two bundles of hand baskets on a carrying rod.*

17. *Basket maker women carry their baskets in delivery bags atop a back basket. Easiest manner of carrying, affording freedom of the hands.*

indeed in all of Europe, as a result of versatility, richness of forms, quality of workmanship as well as invention of types of wares. There is in old Upper Franconian basket weaving a randed linen-bound type of weaving with a particular skein type, the flat skein, which one calls "French" in that area. It is not known whether that weave was developed in Michelau or in France, whether it arose in Upper Franconia for export to France or originated in France itself and was imported into Upper Franconia and from there back to France. Masters' test reports from Braunschweig, for example, state that fine work of "Scheenen", willow skeins, was to be done and displayed. Practical proofs, such as specialized tools, have not yet been found. In general, one had no high opinion of the

114
283–286

unprepossessing but effective and cleverly invented basketmaking tools and threw them away, as was done everywhere.

The lids of Hanseatic servant girls' baskets in Bremen, Hamburg and Luebeck were woven of flat skeins, very firmly but also delicately. These lids were high, so that wine bottles could also be taken out or brought in. The Luebeck type had a pocket in the lid in which visiting cards were kept. The servant girls were judged, hired and paid according to the quality and sturdiness of their hand baskets. Each of the three Hansa cities had its own special type of baskets. Unfortunately, it has not yet been possible

18. *Assortment of contemporary French willow and hand splint baskets, swing baskets and grain bowls.*

19. Handled basket of fine willow skeins. The sieve weave, resembling embroidery, is decorated with colorful yarns, in Biedermeyer style; circa 1840.

20. Handled basket, randed of fine willow skeins, colorfully painted with strong brush strokes; circa 1850.

21. Handbag, close sieve weave, willow skeins decorated with colored wool; circa 1840.

to determine whether these baskets were made by the locals themselves, by Upper Franconian fine basket weavers who moved there, or were all imported from Upper Franconia. It is definite that even before 1945 the last baskets of that type were made in Frohnlach near Coburg and in other towns in that area.

Even today it is still the custom in many parts of Germany to import baskets. That is also true of Austria, where bowl and swing basket makers, "Kirmzainer" (back basket makers) or, formerly, sieve makers from outlying poor regions took the products of their winter work to distant rural areas or cities and into foreign lands. In many regions of West Germany, where basket weaving was practiced in entire villages or districts, in Hessen, in the Weserbergland and in other areas, weaving then died out completely. It was, is and remains an occupation that opposes all intrusions of mechanization, automation and unsuitable rationalization. The last two centuries in particular have clearly shown the decline of basketry and its resurgence in changing times. Good developmental times alternated with weak and poor ones, as around 1860. At that time the basket makers were poor home workers. Only with the further development of basket furniture and the popularity of similar baby carriages did better times again come for the basket makers. It is reported from earlier years that the basket makers, often walking the road from far away carrying their burdens or pushing wheelbarrows, had to wait bareheaded in the courtyards of the merchants, in falling snow, until their work was taken from them and they were given their meager pay. Out of the salary they received they had to buy food and the other necessities of daily life on the spot, so that they usually came home with only a few coins in their pockets. (These conditions were, moreover, one of the main reasons for the long-protracted founding of the Trade School.) Better times came with the victorious war of 1870-71.

When the need for shot baskets increased again with the outbreak of World War I, it drew many people into working at military basket making, without learning more than the simplest weaving. They burdened the occupation in which they stayed or had to stay when military basket making was no longer needed. They did not earn enough, since they lacked the ability, training and mobility to do hard but profitable weaving work. After World War II, especially in the Fifties, there came an unpredictable rise in industry, which brought to the head a whole series of decisive results for basket weaving. Deliveries of woven wares from nonindustrialized countries led, on account of the low salaries then prevailing, to such low prices that the German basket maker could no longer compete. Comparatively low salaries in their own country, in contrast to the many better-paid jobs offered in industry, quickly caused the numbers of active basket makers to decline. On the other hand, this also led to a process of selection and purification in the trade. Everyone who did not have training, ability, knowledge and understanding, capability, practice, strength of will and mastery of weaving techniques to show for himself was swept away. The capable, hardworking, inventive and artistically talented, however, stayed on and created for themselves the means to stay alive. Today, as a result of this development, whole areas of Germany are stripped of basket making activity. In return, the shops are filled with woven wares, mostly of foreign origin.

The Weaving Technique

The Material and its Preparation

Weaving materials exist on every continent, and where no plants thrive there are still animal products. But weaving is very rare in these areas. It is hard to say where the most weaving materials are to be found, where they grow. It is easier to determine where the weaving is finer or coarser, and where it takes place still, again, or for the first time, or no longer or since when. Within the world of nature the plant materials are the most common. The animal and mineral kingdoms offer little. The artificial materials do not approach the growing powers of nature in their secret ways of expression.

The Quantity of Weaving Materials in the World

By "quantity" is meant here the number of plant families and types useful in weaving, as well as the units of weight and pieces of the various types that are usable in weaving. Even the growing, care and reaping of the weaving plants vary considerably. Many plants are found occasionally and only by chance, others such as the basket or cultivated willow must be carefully bred, selected, planted, tended and harvested at a good time. But the number of types of weavable plants is hard to determine. The Trade School in Lichtenfels has a collection of weaving materials, begun new and systematically around 1955, which is, however, arranged only technologically. If one is to differentiate more strictly between weaving plants that can be obtained at regular intervals and in all desired and desirable quantities, and in the quality needed for large-scale production in the basket industry, and those that are only used occasionally by amateurs or in small workshops, only in one place or in a small area, then the first type can be summed up quickly, the others not at all.

The Weaving Value of Plant Materials

Weaving is actually built on the tensile strength and carrying power of the reeds and skeins. That is true of all types of limited weaves. The hung weaves depend on the very flexible thin and tough fibers and thus are similar to women's handicrafts such as crocheting, knitting and hooking. We see flexible withstanding power not only in a straw of grain, but most of all in willows during a storm. This limited ability to give way and ever-returning tensile strength are in the nature of the wood. With willows, as with the Scotch pine tree, every individual rod, every stem in a close clump must strive toward the light, so as not to be choked by its neighbors. So it must stand straight up or always be able to right itself. This willingness to stretch remains in the wood when it is cut and, so to speak, dead. In just this way the firmness of the weave is maintained. In this ability always to retain these qualities, in heat or cold, even amid some dampness, there lies the high use value of the weaving plants.

Nomenclature of Plants Suitable for Weaving

The German language lacks a unified nomenclature for the plants or plant parts used in weaving. So it is not possible here to name one really good word for the shapes and forms of materials ready for weaving, a word that would designate, describe and fit everything equally and inclusively at the same time. If one speaks of the "willowy" nature of a weaving material, for example, then on the basis of the name it should apply only to the willow. The "skein condition" that also has the job of defining the condition of round and barked materials is an expression that actually defines only a certain cutting preparation of the willow or hazel, and yet it must be used inclusively, although there are many cut forms. One should regard this list of designations as the forms in which the raw weavable or prepared parts of weaving plants appear:

1. **Weide:** willow, as a rod, a switch.
2. **Gerte:** switch, used as a rod.
3. **Rute:** rod, for willow, hazel and other slim twigs or sprouts.
4. **Stock:** stick, of great strength, of willows in their second or third year of growth.
5. **Stab:** stave, not much different from a stick: wood stave, round stave.
6. **Stecken:** staff; see stave and stick.

7. **Stengel:** stem, of weaker plants, herbs, orchids.

8. **Stamm:** trunk, a stick of many years' growth, or at least a thick one, for splintwood and also for tools.

9. **Spalte:** split, a half to a quarter of a rod. 10. Schieve:

10. **Schiene:** skein, a split rod, compressed, planed, slimmed.

11. **Scheene or Schaene:** a skein in North German dialects.

12. **Spliete, Spleisse:** likewise North German: split (willow or hazel).

13. **Span:** splint, a strip or skein removed by hand from annular rings or taken off radially.

14. **Leiste:** fillet, a thicker, smoothed skein or prepared softwood.

15. **Halm:** straw, a grass, straw or palm-leaf blade etc.

16. **Stiel:** stalk, in rare cases a leaf stalk, such as that of the cocoa palm.

17. **Band:** band, in recent years a rattan band, like a splint.

18. **Faden:** ribbon, rattan ribbon, thin (ribbon rattan) in the case of round rattan.

19. **Strang:** line, multiple-fibered thin, weak material.

20. **Streifen:** strip, used by Dr. Lehmann to systematize weavers.

21. **Straehne:** strain, of very thin, fine materials, also hairs, in masses.

22. **Wulst:** roll, a weft for spiral work, with one or more parts.

23. **Schnur:** string, of rush, or drilled out of thin blades of straw, turned.

24. **Scheit:** billet, a split trunk piece prepared with right angles, above all in splint weaving, for cutting or planing to a splint.

25. **Borte:** edge, a flattened braid of multiple strains of straw, reed, cattail.

26. **Kordel:** cord, thinner than string, more twisted, more three-dimensional, as of reeds.

27. **Stammstuecke:** trunk pieces, such as block, log, lath, fillet, board, as an early stage of making splints.

28. **Stake:** stake, a type used in building baskets (rib, upsetter, spoke).

All the named forms of materials ready to weave can be used as stakes, weavers, winding or binding materials, each according to its suitability; some in multiple ways, some in one. A collective name for this does not exist.

Efforts to Discover new Natural Weaving Materials

The Spaniards one brought back from the Far East a reed which became known as the "Spanish reed", [69, 70] particularly in reference to a strict manner of education. It was the palm reed, the climbing palm of East Asia. That is the first provable case of importing new materials from other lands. And even today a certain stiff grass from Sardinia is exported to Elba and Ischia, where the fishermen use it to weave their weirs etc., as they did in olden days.

With the rise of a real basket industry in Upper Franconia, it soon became necessary to import new weaving materials, natural ones (as also artificial ones, textiles) from outside, in order to attain variations of quickly made and therefore cheap weaves of the simplest kind. In the Seventies and Eighties of the last century, many new materials were sought and found by the Michelau basket firm of Georg Gagel, through trips made [22–26] for that purpose. The so-called Esparto, on the other hand, that had been introduced from Southern Europe around 1840, died out by the turn of the century and is no longer obtainable.

For the layman and the small business there remained, as before, the wild plants not used by the basket industry, parts of garden plants, such as the stalks of certain decorative grasses, also their leaves, the stems of lily plants etc. that are also usable as materials.

Materials Occurring Naturally in Large Quantities

Rod-forming plants: rods can always be used whole or split and planed. The most important native German rod plant is the willow. It occurs:

a) as cultivated willow in closely planted beds, called willow cultures or willow gardens. The close growing [62–65] makes for straight stems and high growth.

b) as half-wild head willows, planted for the most part by farmers along brooks to secure the shore; the rods of them are cut off in lengths of more than a man's height. Head [63] willows grow in various lands to various head heights.

c) as bush or shrub willows. They are not used for weaving, because they are too branched, but can be put to good use by laymen, especially for the smaller types of basket weaving, such as for doll houses or Christmas mangers, using the finest twigs and branches. The [232] outstanding basket maker Wagner in Schammelsberg [235] near Bayreuth raised his own shrub willows in the woods, harvesting from them the long thin twigs for his "Coburg" carrying baskets.

d) as tree willows with a long branchless stem (sallow, from salix, willow). It provides excellent weaving material as a result of its thick and yet light wood. It is not easy to

23. Sack basket with turned wooden bells.

24. Pastry bowl with braided stakes and folded rim.

25. Man's summer hat, fine willow skein work. Often inscribed "Greetings!"; the last read "Farewell!".

26. Handbag, twilled and randed skeins, two-tone pairing. (23-26 from the Gagel catalog.)

22. Title page of the catalog of the Gagel Co., circa 1839, chalk drawing on stone. Both main buildings now belong to the German Basket Museum. The family business was founded in 1803. The shipping crates in the picture already indicate overseas trade of the finest woven goods.

splint, but provides the finest and smoothest hand splints. There is now only one "Braschelmacher" in the small market town of Marktgraitz near Lichtenfels. "Braschel" are, in the Upper Franconian dialect, the sallow or palm willow splints that were used in the Mitwitz area for making very small baskets.

Hazel rods are tough, splittable and peelable. Other stick growths, of the privet, the buckthorn, and the sweet chestnut, are also good for small uses.

The willow, though, is the queen of Central European weaving plants because of its beauty and manifold uses.

The splint-providing woods form a small science of their own. The finest kind of splint, the toughest, the loveliest, is the hand splint, which can be taken in many ways. The carefully chosen trunk is sawn into blocks one to two meters long. These are split into radial pieces with iron and wood wedges. Finally the pieces are cut into right-angled logs on the sawbuck, in order to obtain

80–84

splints as equally wide as possible; then the splints are drawn off them in varying widths, an art it takes several years to learn.

Pine can be named as one of the best splint-providing woods, but a suitable type does not grow everywhere. In certain wooded regions around Bamberg, a half sandy but in places also swampy stretch of land, is found an excellent splint pine.

The shiny surface of the hand splint of the pine or Scotch pine, taken off between the wood (the actual growth of the annular ring) and the growth layer (cambium), is inimitable and not attainable through any artificial means. Especially suitable pines, that have grown poorly in sandy soil in dry years, give paper-thin splints. The splints are taken off both with the annular rings and radially, that is, from the bark to the center. That is done chiefly when one wants shingles whose grooves lead rain water away quickly, or when one is to make sieve frames and splint boxes that require very wide splints. The width of the concentric annular-ring splints is not great. Other splint-providing woods are spruce, fir, larch, oak, poplar, aspen, ash and a few rarely-used types that are used, for example, in the Bavarian Woods or in the area around Stilfs in South Tirol, the sallow, walnut etc. Besides hand-removed splints there are also the so-called esparto splints. They were prepared in the former Sudetenland in the town of Alt-Ehrenberg and used for the finest flat weaves of limited size (for example, hat linings, linings for mailboxes etc.). Russian linden or aspen, both with very thick, light, resin-free wood, are cut into billets, then prepared by long softening in a special lye, and planed down with big two-man planes, with blade widths up to six centimeters, generally under cracks in the smooth billet, to slim straws or splints. (This technique may also be dying out.)

The willow plane splint is made when strong rods or willow stakes are split and planed down with a hand plane (or a planing machine). Between the rod or stake skeins that form parts of a circle a splint can also come off, which unlike the actual willow skein is rather rough and is used for the bottom weave of cheap baskets. The hazel splint is produced in similar manner, removed likewise by the stamping ram and then smoothed with a willow plane or even over the knee and planed. In Thuringia fine weaving of hazel splints, with or without the growth layer, was carried on until about 1941, with excellent results. Knife veneer splints can provide good weavable splints of soft, thick, even woods such as the brown willow, and many hardwoods are also suited to it. The wide veneer sheets must then be cut down into weaving strips. Even in early days knife veneer was used for basket weaving by the bowl makers of Emsdetten instead of the radial splints of the brown willow, which were hard to remove; this inspired the way of using knife veneer strips often practiced today in Upper Franconia.

Peeled veneer, generally cut off one- to one-and-a-half-meter-long blocks of poplar trunks in spirals, as if from a roll of paper, provides endless courses of thin veneer that can be cut into weaving strips. This type is known from the long, right angled fruit crates with wide splint handles, and is only good for packing cases. Root splints made of spruce or larch roots are also used, the former in Franconia and the Bavarian Woods, the latter in the mountains, especially in South Tirol. The removal of root splints requires much practice, as does all splint work, and is scarcely practical for the layman. Spruce root splints are very excellent; they are the toughest weaving material to be found in the country for stronger baskets, particularly those that require tensile strength. The making of spruce root splints, moreover, usually involves difficulties; to be sure, spruce grows in the woodland glades of farmers, who are happy when the basket weaver digs it out, as it is a nuisance to them. But the forester is opposed to it, for the roots hold and nourish the spruces at the edge of the forest. Their removal is illegal. The long roots are split or pulled off and the root skeins worked into back baskets and, above all, swing baskets, bowls and basins. There is nothing that can replace them.

Thread-forming growths: by "threads" the basket weaver means plant stems, small stalks, that areslim, as uniformly thin as possible, long and above all windable, but also the thin round rattan fibers.

The wild grape, a climbing plant that climbs high on host plants in thick brush and can, unlike other weaving plants, be pulled down in very long pieces, is used peeled or barked. It is especially suitable as an inlay for not too rough spiral roll work.

The wild grape and the hop vine fulfill similar purposes. They are not as smooth and fine as the lordly willow. They are all suitable for weaving over strong stakes, such as full willows or hazel rods. The knots of the barked or peeled wild grape liven up a weave, giving it a native air.

The tubes: the reed, common in Germany along rivers and ponds and in swampy regions, belongs, like the South European canna or arrundo with its many strong stalks, and the bamboo that grows to forty meters and even higher, to the grasses. All have knots with dividing walls. In general they can be bent only with difficulty, but can be split, even planed, so that through knee planing their grooves become flat skeins and can be woven. The reed can still be used well for making artistic writing and drawing pens, along with all the other uses that it serves.

One finds the toughest reeds in areas with iron-rich soil. It should be cut in times of frost and ice. In the Upper Franconian basket industry, and among German basket makers in general, it finds no use, while in Southern Europe, especially in Italy and Spain, it is used freely.

77   The hollow wood of the elderberry, freshly cut, is rather soft, but turns as hard as bone. The Thuringian basket weavers use this unusual wood to make their hand planes.

Soft slim plant stems and leaves: it is not necessary for all weaving purposes to use only hard, stiff, rigid materials. In addition to even-surfaced mats to cover floors and walls, there are also baskets and pouches, for example shopping bags, for which a certain softness and flexibility are desirable, such as is particularly native to rushes.

The rushes grow on river and pond shores in fresh water, but also, as on the Friesian Islands in the Netherlands, in the sea, where the battle against storm and salt water makes them grow firmer, tougher and more windable than the well-protected freshwater rushes. The round smooth stem, that also takes the place of green leaves, is filled with spongy air chambers that help the rushes to float well in high water. Out of them the Indians of Lake Titicaca weave, bind and roll their artistic boats, and the Sards their half-boats that are only one rush long.

The wood rushes, actually Simsen, look like miniature rushes in appearance and posture; they prefer damp and shaded places in the woods and grow to be about sixty centimeters high, while the pond rushes reach over two meters, more than a man's height. When harvested at the right time, they can be woven, particularly as rolled inlays for the finer spiral work. The Hydrobiological Institute in Ploen (Dr. Kaethe Seidl) has particularly taken up the job of researching the growing and weaving of rushes.

The cattails, the wide- and narrow-leafed types, are known for their thin, smooth, round and regular stems, on which the blossoms and, in their brown club form, the fruit heads grow. The stems are not used in weaving, but the long, even, sword-shaped leaves that come out of the water separately can be woven smoothly or combined in plaits or edgings. Excellent pouches of this material come today from the East European states, well done in their construction, proportions and use of material. The Rumanian Danube lowlands, for example, are rich in rushes, cattails and other such growths. The cattails were formerly used for the "Verlieschen" of barrels, the thickening of the barrel bottoms.

Artificial materials: metallic and half-metallic bands and edgings were often used in the 1880's, a time of well-to-do ostentation, without any good effect on the formation and mastery of the weaver's material. Rather the creative powers of the handicraft were thereby lost.

Nor have chemical weaving materials been able to maintain themselves in opposition to the natural ones. They are better suited to other purposes. For example, the soft plastic strands supplied by Rehau Plastics are very 119–130 useful as research material, especially for the invention, testing and systematic realization of stake borders, and cannot be done without in such areas. They allow many patterns to be developed, through the application and variation of numbers, they can be woven in any form and, particularly in the testing, forming and deforming of patterns, be put to similar use again immediately.

There are very excellent artificial materials, such as polyethylene. Saleen is also very much like natural weaving material, but always requires special training in working it.

Half-fabrications: by this term is meant in basket weaving all ties, plaits, edgings and cords produced by weaving natural weaving plants, for the most part woven bands that in themselves have been plaited one or more times. Straw edgings have become very common, such as were woven in early times by women in mountainous woodlands with little arable land and long winters, for example the Black Forest and the Swiss Aargau. Cattail braids were made, especially in Bohemia, and were much worked in Upper Franconia and sewn into many-colored mats and rugs. Bohemia had the best cattails. The place where a weaving plant grows is, as has been said, of great importance. In Michelau cattails—particularly hand-woven reed plaits of from three to five strands—were run through wooden rollers much like laundry mangles, though smaller in size, in order to make thin, broad edgings. Strings of reeds, laid rather than drilled by experts, were not often seen. They took on their pearly appearance from expert turning strokes.

Obtaining weaving plants has already been discussed. Their extent is simply incalculable. There are material plants growing in Germany as well as in other countries, near or far, such as the willow. Until the last war they were grown almost exclusively in Germany for German basket makers and worked in homeland workshops. Many large willow plantations, comprising thousands of hectares, in the Oder lowlands around Breslau and Brieg, fell to Poland after the war. From then on willows were imported from there into West Germany at such low prices that the German willow growers were compelled to give up their willow plantations completely, all the more so for lack of personnel with knowledge of farming and forestry, and even the willow farmers who moved from West Prussia and Silesia to Franconia had to uproot their plantations and grow sugar beets. But when the German willow plantations were gone, the price of imported willow suddenly rose sharply, and in the end foreign lands naturally realized that more was to be earned by exporting their willows to Germany in the form of finished wares. Now the native basket weaver could no longer make ends meet, and people working in the basket industry were at times compelled to switch to other industrial occupations. To be sure, there is still willow cultivation in Germany, but it is too little for the constant need, aside from the fact that many willow growers weave their harvests themselves.

Good weaving straw, too, can scarcely be had any more. Grain is grown very short today, thus it is unusable for rolled straw weaving. When straw still grew long and grain fields stood taller than a man's height, straw weavers could cut off the grain heads with a scythe and obtain the best weaving straw. Flail threshing, even by the now very old-fashioned wide threshing machine, still provided long, readily weavable straw. But the combine harvester damages the straw so much that it is no longer usable. Today it must, like basket willow, be imported.

Fresh-water reeds grow in Germany, and reed weavers today are still familiar with North Germany's many types of weaving and roofing reeds. Birch twigs, which are scarcely woven nowadays, can be had in ample quantities, but nobody wants them. Fine woodland grasses, such as the hair grasses that grow in woodland clearings or mountain forests, can be used well in rolled wefts, especially for fine spiral work, but in Germany today it is mainly amateurs who carry on the tedious though not strenuous work of spiral weaving. In Austria's Burgenland, and particularly in Styria, farmers still weave very beautiful and fine straw baskets of all kinds in winter, even though the admirable big storage baskets have almost died out there.

Foreign Weaving Materials used in Germany

The palm leaf belongs among these. Nobody knows today whether the time-consuming palm-leaf work will ever again be taken up in the Upper Franconian woodland villages of the Frankenwald near the Thuringian, or formerly Thuringian territory. But the amateur weaver, who does not have to struggle to earn a living with his weaving, can make very good use of the palm leaf. It should not cause great difficulties to obtain foreign palm leaves, except from Cuba, which exports none at this time, but rather from countries which have always made beautiful and not too hard-to-make woven goods of them. The techniques of palm-leaf weaving are scarcely known to us. The spiral roll work practiced in Upper Franconia with palm-leaf fronds over round cross-section stakes of

rattan is also very common in foreign lands, especially among the Amerindians, but there are countless other types of weaving with palm leaves, which we would first have to learn by doing them. Strips cut in equal widths can be very useful to the amateur in particular types of work, as in reed, cattail, birchbark and wood splint (Swedish splint) techniques.

Sea grass (esparto) is not very simple to use. Straw edgings of it were imported very cheaply and in excellent quality from China for decades, because through the industrialization of the German-speaking lands the weaving of edging as a home occupation has been given up.

China rush string could also be imported again today for many kinds of weaving, both crude and attractive uses, even if it were only done in small quantities for the work of laymen. Bamboo, or the bamboo tube, used in a remarkable variety of ways in East Asian lands, as a vegetable as well as for temple flower baskets, for flower vases as well as house building, can be worked by us only with difficulty, for it reaches us very hardened after long ocean voyaging. Attempts to make bamboo into fine splints and skeins have thereby been ruled out, aside from amateur and hobby activity. The fine techniques of bamboo preparation and use are still so highly developed in the old Oriental cultures, haveso permeated the flesh and blood of the workers who live there, that what could be done here would be clumsy in comparison. Even the hundreds of types of bamboo are inaccessible to us. The Tonkin reed, a type of bamboo, is used by us merely for gardening purposes, because it is tough and scarcely rots. The palm reed, the climbing palm (*calamus rotang*), is almost the only one of all the foreign weaving plants used in chair-cane factories in Germany. Here too a change has taken place. While even shortly before the last war there were four such chair-cane factories in Hamburg, Bergedorf, Bremen and Grub-am-Forst, near Coburg, today only the last-named factory is still working with many varieties of rattan that are imported via the Netherlands. Hong Kong and Indonesia are already working the rotang palm by machine, so that it is almost cheaper to import rattan from from East Asia than to prepare it here.

In the case of the "palm reed" we are not talking of an actual reed, a grass type in the botanical sense, but rather a climbing palm. In its best form it grows in what was once part of Indonesia and is now Malaysia, on the islands of the Malay Archipelago, in the jungles there and to some extent also in plantations near villages. With gripping arms and tendrils like those of the wild grape it climbs up host trees and reaches lengths of up to 180 meters. The good quality and excellent usability of the approximately 400 types of rattan is due to their hard fight for life in the

25

warm, moist jungles, their fight for light, as was said of the willows and maples. As protection against many kinds of parasites, the slim, willowy, always equally thick plant has a strong bark equipped with many spines or thorns. Among them is the so-called "Peddig" which is attached to the bark by a growth layer which thickens to a glassy skin of silicic acid against the wood. Above all, it gives the wood the strength to withstand parasites. The underground rootstock has many branches, constantly puts out shoots in new locations, and lies quite horizontally under the ground. The diameter of the even stems, according to the type and variety, ranges from a thinness of 5 mm to a thickness of about 60 mm. In the jungles the natives remove the thorny bark from the stems to about a man's height above the ground and pull them down from the trees. The pieces, three to six meters long, are then sorted, freed of resin over a fire and straightened. In the storage areas, which usually lie along raftable rivers, they are cleaned with water and sand, dried and tied in bundles. Bundled by numbers or weight, they are now taken for export to the seaports, after which they are sometimes named. In addition to Singapore, the main shipping ports are those on the southeast coast of Borneo and Macassar (Celebes).

Because its glossy skin layer is impervious to liquids, the natural reed is not easy to dye and is therefore woven uncolored. But since the ochre-tinged basic color always varies a bit, since in fact the natural tones, when varnished, vary through the whole spectrum, with yellowish, greenish, bluish, reddish and violet tints, the lively unfinished use is most congenial for home use. According to the glassy skin layers they have, the natural reeds are called glossy or half-glossy reeds. The soft, often bleached reeds have been more or less completely freed of their glass skin by washing with water and sand and soaking in a thinned fluoric acid that removes the glass. The three main types, glossy, half-glossy and the little used Telt reed, occur in hundreds of useful forms. Most of them are known by technical names, according to their uses. Many names, like that of the very thin (about 5 mm in diameter), very colorful Bondut reed (spelled Boondout in Dutch), are of Malay origin.

The whole undivided reeds can also be united for use as framing reeds, such as the dark brown Malacca reed of 16 to 32 mm thickness, the bright and even-colored Manila reed of 8 to 45 mm thickness, the very knotty Manau reed of 16 to 60 mm thickness, which because of the black rings at its knots (shoots) and the dark brown places where insects have eaten at it, has a very foreign appearance. Among the weaker reeds, that serve better for weaving than for framing, are among others the basket reed with a great variety of types, the aforementioned

Bondut, the once frequently used beater reed, very tough varieties that were used to make countless rug beaters in Upper Franconia. But there are also many other types, which vary in part through botanical relationship, in part through their different growth.

The classes of rattan quality in general are established and defined according to color, hardness, firmness, evenness, surface and bleaching treatment, as well as more minute differences. The types are recognized by their so-called band colors, that is, by particularly colored strands, according to which one can at once recognize and compare types and prices. Since they are natural products, it is not possible to sort and ship them to exact specifications. The long sea voyage, for example, can cause running in the reed if it was loaded while damp.

European importing ports are Hamburg, Bremen, Amsterdam, Rotterdam, Le Havre and Genoa.

The peeling products of the natural reeds are likewise very numerous. In making good natural reed skeins, the chair-cane factories use the best original types as "machine reeds", above all equally strong and knot-free ones that can be put through the machine easily. Among the peeling products are those whose choice and use as machine reeds are successful mainly because of the rind, the glass skin layer, as with chair-plaiting and weaving reeds, but also others, of which only the interior of the reed, the rattan, is sought and the peel is only a by-product that can be turned to cash. In preparing the various types of reed skeins, as well as the rattans, in many forms, the natural reed stems have to be carefully sought, washed, sorted, trimmed (freed of knot growths), and straightened. The trimming or smoothing of the knot growths, like all the other work, must be done by experienced and practiced specialists. For example, to prepare natural cane skeins in semi-circular form, the natural reed is cut along its length into equal sections by special very hard knives as it goes through the machine, and then machined again by jet knives that cut off the glass skin and leave a three- to eight-sided stake. These raw skeins with their glass skin layer are planed and slimmed down to very fine ones within 1/100 mm.

Peeled products exist in many forms. The chair plaiting cane has served since about the middle of the Seventeenth Century for weaving wooden objects with a weave of six-or eight-sided holes. Chair plaiting weave is the most expensive product of the chair-cane factories. The wrapping cane is wider, reaching a width of up to 10 mm, and is used both for wrapping basket furniture and weaving an endless variety of patterns. The reed bast is a useful by-product of rattan making. Because of its toughness it is very often used today to weave swing baskets and bowls with hand splint borders. Edging by-products, such as the

27. Stick basket of willow skeins, pincushion and decorative border of red felt with silk trimming, octagonal weave, Michelau, circa 1880.

28. Mending basket, white full willows and brightly dyed willow skeins. Top with twill weave decorations, crossed border, strengthening hoop on the top, bound crosswise, common for many decades, until about 1930, Hessian Schwalm area. Leter reproduced until about 1940 in the Lichtenfels area.

29. *Wrapped straw roll work, upper part decorated with colored straw above, Egypt, circa 1950.*

30.*basket-round wrapped straw roll work with lively natural colors. Below: fruit bowl (or something similar) of spiral work, decorated as in #29, hoops decorating the border are broken off! Both from Central Africa.*

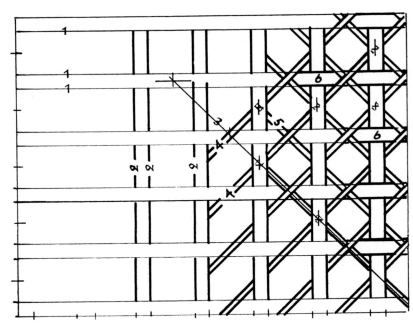

31. *Cane chair weave, called octagonal weave, introduced from East Asia and adopted, immovable structure, rich in geometrical figures, variable in many ways (width, thickness, proportion, intervals etc.).*

32. *Formation of a weave pattern drawing.*

polished reeds, are also worked.

The German name of the Rattan reed, "Peddig", comes from Dutch. Rattans are used according to their quality, color, cross-section, shape and thickness. Among them, as also with natural reeds and peeled products, there are commercial wares that are standardized and always available, substandard wares that sometimes result from natural conditions, and finally special preparations that are made only in profitable quantities. Rattan is also sold in large long bundles as well as in small quantities, known as rings, for laymen, while the long, once-bent bundles that are classified by color go to large consumers. Besides the natural-colored rattans, there are also the bleached types, which yellow strongly with age and thus can scarcely be used for artistic creations.

The most common round rattans with circular cross-sections are sold according to thickness, as reed number 0000 of 0.18 mm to number 8 of 3 mm diameter. The

70

thicker ones, known as stake reeds, go from 3.25 mm to 4.75 mm, while the diameter in hundredths of a millimeter is also used as a numerical designation. The thick stave rattans exist in diameters from 5 to 12 mm and more. Flat skeins can be had in widths of 4 to about 6 mm; the wider ones, very good for use in full-blooded, rhythmically composed weaves, usually are prepared specially. The rattan bands of flat right-angled cross-section are made in various widths, thicknesses and proportions; this allows a considerable increase in the array of weaving patterns. Special profiles, such as triangles, squares etc., are to be had only by special order. They are used mainly in construction and decorative weaving. Rattan can be bought ready to weave and worked favorably after a few minutes of wetting and softening, which makes it especially suitable for amateur work.

267   Rattan can be dyed, smoked, stained, sulphurated and bleached. India-rubber lacquers of particular holding and flexing power create colorful covering finishes with genuine light mineral colors. The first lacquer reeds, about 1840, were rattan skeins, finished only with polished black shellac, so that the natural grain was still visible. Today they are clear and highly glossy. We have lacquered reed staves of round stake reeds, lacquered reed skeins of rattan skein, lacquered bands of soft rattan or cording, and there also used to be lacquered bands of very flat thin rattan.

Burning and Bending Natural Reeds and Rattans

Soft rattans bend after light softening, without creasing. Rattan stakes have to be warmed over a gentle flame and bent immediately. After they cool quickly, which can be hastened with a damp cloth, the bend remains, especially if it was burned long enough and bent a bit too far. Burning requires practice, experience and complete composure, plus great strength and a fine sensitivity to the conditions inside the reed.

Weaving materials like linden and raffia bast are of no significance today, as they are either unavailable or lack firmness.

Weaving Plants Grown and Utilized only in Other Countries

68   The Southern European-Sardinian "Arrundo" is related
85   to the Sardinian hard rush, which grows over a meter high and is very tough. The "Mazzolano", a native type of straw and grain that grows in Italy, especially in Tuscany near Florence, and that can be cut into edgings and woven

splendidly and also made into baskets, is known in Germany as ripstraw ("Reissstroh", not to be confused with "Reisstroh", rice straw).

The sweet chestnut is found, to be sure, in the southern Palatinate, but in such small numbers that it is insignificant for weaving. But in Tessin and Northern Italy, as far as Umbria, it thrives in forest stands, and the fallen chestnuts that are not harvested grow into new shoots, similar to willow rods, that can be woven well. The more mature stems are splinted. From the younger wood in particular one gets striped splints which are very decorative in and of themselves. The simple but professional-quality baskets have a very lively effect. The stripes from the young stems provide a congenial natural ornamentation in even the simplest randing weaves. The North Italian and Swiss carrying baskets of spirited form are more unified in color.

Birch bark should also be mentioned, likewise the types of palm leaves, of which the Sardinian dwarf palm is the   163–16 most tropical type growing in Europe. In Sardinia excellent basket wares are made of its leaves. In the tropical lands, especially in East Asia, South America and Africa, the long slim fronded leaves of palms are cut into   384 fine and extra-fine strips and worked into natural-colored and colorful dyed works of art. In the Philippines the leaf   115 ribs of the cocoa palm are woven like round rattan. Bamboo also belongs to this group. Its high silicic acid   113 content (which the oak and the palm reed also produce) makes it tough and durable.

For many kinds of work there are grasses and reeds of excellent firmness and often fine thinness all over the world. Of them the finest and smallest "eye-pleasing" weaves are made. The number of their types is unknown, as are also plants that either do not come into our area or cannot be recognized when woven.

The ways of packing weaving plants that come from foreign lands are very fascinating. Often there are mats   66 and full weavings in strange shapes. Bamboo also has to be packed with thick coverings to avoid too quick drying.

The weaving material trade in Upper Franconia: In   71 order to meet the very great need for weaving materials, the basket material trade developed early along the upper Main, and had the job of gathering great loads of native and, especially, foreign weaving materials and making them available to the retail trade and the workshops. The change in trade methods, the buyers' tastes and the other developments in the basket industry required a constant assortment in the storerooms, until the aforementioned decline of basket making forced this commerce into many changes.

The Nomenclature of The Materials

The Names of Weaving Plants in the German Language

There is as yet no complete dictionary of all willow names. The science of the salix species, the types of willow, is difficult, both linguistically and botanically, as the willow is quite the problem child of the botanists. The dioecious willow is as good for crossing as it is for cultivation. Its identifying marks of root types, withes, stems, twigs, buds, leaves, fruit, bark, wood, color and shape, as well as its appearance as the seasons change, its growth and wilting, are so varied in a botanical as well as a weaving sense that the line between minor growth variations and genuine varieties or easily separable species and types is very fine, and includes a wide threshold of transitions. There are not too many names used by those who cultivate it, but Latin designations, High German or dialect names are as numerous as they are confusing.

False Names: particular types turn up and stick in one's mind. One does not proceed very scientifically with a people whose conceptualization is strict but unpictorical and abstract when it comes to giving names. One prefers word pictures as exact as possible, for example, for the Cuban palm leaf that was much worked in the Upper Franconian towns of Mitwitz, Hassenberg and Gestungshausen. The single fronded leaves, once out of their accordion-folded state when packed, have approximately the form of reed leaves, which are also long, narrow and sword-shaped, particularly cattail leaves. So the home folks simply called the palm leaf "Schilf" (reed).

Willow tops were originally the too-thin tips of the whole willow rods left after weaving, or the tips cut off before splitting the whole rods, likewise because they were too thin. But the very short yet steel-tough weaving willows once imported from England and later from the French Jura were "tops", English or French tops, although they were whole willows, from butt end to the finest tip, from poor growths of up to about 60 cm high.

The raffia or raphia bast is not a genuine bast in the scientific sense. It is the outer skin of the fronded leaves of the raffia-ruffia palm from Madagascar, that easily comes loose from the rotting inner part through "rusting", soaking in warm ponds, and that survives its rotting because of its greater silicic acid content. Likewise the reed bast that we mentioned is a peeling product and has nothing to do with the thin bast, which exists between the bark and the growth or acid layer of the linden tree. Rattan reed is not a reed, but clearly a stem wood, though with countless hair tubes which run up to the fronded top. A leaf of the raffia-ruffia palm, moreover, is up to ten meters long; the single fronds can almost reach two meters.

The "China rush string" was known in Upper Franconia as "Elba string", the name given it by the Danish firm of L. & H., which first imported it. One might also recall the "Ullbrich willow", a breed created by the Director of the Berlin Botanical Museum, Dr. Ullbrich, who made himself very useful in the world of weaving plants.

Specialized terms connected with "willow" are especially numerous; here we can mention only willow cultivation, cultured willow, weaving willow, split willow, upsett willow, head willow, layer willow, layer wood, cube willow, body willow, willow skein work, willow basket, imperial willow, pussy willow etc.

Similarly, specialized terms with "rattan" or "palm reed" are common: ribbon rattan, staff rattan, skein rattan, three-cornered rattan, red or blue band rattan, rattan skeins, rattan band, rattan weaving, reed bast, palm reed, lacquered reed, Spanish reed etc.

Tools-Utensils-Machines

The Basket Weaver's Hand as a Tool

When one emphasizes repeatedly that basket weaving is a handicraft, then the hand must be significantly effective and versatile in it. That is particularly true of the hand's gripping techniques. Among basket weavers, the willow splitter and splint remover must have trained their hands especially well. Both activities demand a fine degree of equilibrium, tension and loosening in succession without cramping, without false and superhuman straining. The basket maker constantly feels his willows with his hand, his fingers. One may also consider what the weaver can do with just his awl, making holes for tying, increasing spaces, rolling skein ends into spirals, pressing them together in fitches, using the awl, so to speak, as a striking iron, smoothing out unevenness with the awl held flat, tearing out clumps with the sharp point, splitting needles, driving the awl into the workbench to hold the bottom while he opens it out, reversing the awl and knocking willows down into place with the handle, and so on. In a similar sense the whole hand, as a closed fist, is a hammer, a mallet, a cudgel. The edge of the hand often takes the place of the rapping iron or wood, knocking the weft, that is, the laid-in and woven-in willows, tightly together. The edge of the hand takes over, saving time and effort, especially with thin willows or a weave of soft materials.

The hand also works as a pincer that holds or, if necessary, squeezes things together. A willow, for example, can be gripped, held and moved between the strongest fingers, the thumb and index finger. The fingernails form pliers or cutters, they serve as tearing nails or in place of a pencil. The cupped fingers and the heel of the hand help out in gripping, holding and squeezing like a vise; the raw split willow is held by the palm, thumb and four fingers while being planed down.

Both hands together form a bending tool, in that they grasp, hold and also bend strongly together. In simple weaving the left hand holds down the weavers that are already in place, the right hand weaves and winds the weaver through the stakes. A stick is bent over the knee with both hands when laid under. To bend the stronger sticks evenly, the basket maker has a bending wood or iron. But for that too he needs both hands, the left to hold and the right to grip and press.

Ripping or separating, splitting willows, can be done if necessary by two fingers and a thumb. The straight index finger can be used as a borer or awl when a space must be pressed into a loose weave to pass a ring or the like through.

The thumbnail serves best as a scratcher, a peeler, when it is necessary to scratch a bit of the bark or some other spot off the gleaming bare wood. It is plain, though, that only soft weaving wood gives in willingly to the thumb. The bent index finger, another, or several fingers together act as a hook to pull loops or knots out of the weave. The fingertips serve for touching, feeling, pushing or measuring. The maker of fine baskets needs fingertip feeling, for he measures the thickness of his willow skeins not with a mechanical measuring instrument, but between two fingertips, because thus fineness, smoothness, thickness and resistance, firmness when bent and the necessary bending pressure in a process can be determined. Steel measuring instruments, because of their hardness, are too rough on soft skeins.

The hand is also of great importance as a measuring instrument, a ruler. The arrangement of the material maintains its regularity, down to the finest mathematical-geometrical exactness and strictness. With rough and unevenly formed material it would be senseless to try to maintain a precision of fractions of a millimeter, not only because the weaving wood would oppose it, but also because overdone precision is not needed for hay, leaf and manure baskets and their contents that do not need protection. On the other hand, for fine table utensils neatness, also in the evenness of the weave, is naturally the rule all over the world.

The thumb itself, like the slimmer fingers if need be, serves to measure medium widths, and at 2.4 cm equals an inch. The length of a finger can be used similarly. The distance between the tips of the thumb and little finger is an old unit of measure, the handspan. The ell, measured from the elbow to the tip of the middle finger, is not just a tailor's measure for cloth. Finally, the span of the outstretched arms is a measurement in old usage among back basket makers. It represents the whole exact limit needed in free-hand weaving. By it, for example, the spokes (ribs, stakes) of the back-borne "Kerm" baskets are measured.

The Tools of Basket Making

As the weaver needs no machines, or only very crude ones, to prepare his materials, he also has no need of machine tools for their application. His hand remains his most important tool, supported by comparatively few hand-held tools. A saw, perhaps a bow saw, is used not only to saw off thick, hard sticks, for which the basket maker's shears are not sufficient. It also serves not only for cutting, slitting and splitting hard sticks, but also for cutting in while bending the handle of a basket, which is made of a spruce bough or a thick hazel stick. The branches that are peeled and sometimes smoothed a bit for that purpose are softened and then bent. But since the sharp bending of thick branches cannot be achieved through softening alone, cuts are sawn into the inside of the bow at close intervals, almost to the middle of the diameter. Thus the actual inner length of the bow is diminished by the cumulative breadth of the saw blade. It no longer supports and braces itself against the compressing pressure on the inside of the bow.

The locksmith's hammer, a good practical tool available in many sizes and weights, gives good service for general use in basket weaving. The actual fine basket maker's hammer resembles the saddler's; it has a small round or square head and a wide thin claw.

At the Lichtenfels Trade School experiments were made in improving the basket maker's shears in terms of gripping, forging and cutting as well as securing. The basket weaver also uses files for wood and metal and wood rasps, as well as the usual types of needle-nose and cutting pliers with which fastening nails are removed. The side cutters used in weaving, with a special set of blades, are a fine development of the usual everyday side cutters; their blades are set so that they can work very close to the weave, in order to snip projecting ends and knots of the willows off neatly. The tools generally made by the village blacksmith according to the basket maker's requirements, like many farming and craft tools, had letters and numbers cut into them. They lasted more than a lifetime. The Trade School's tool collection includes an individually made striking-bending awl of the master basket maker Boettner, who came to Lichtenfels from Thuringia; it is a unique combination of several tools in one. Through it the work

bench, the array of tools, was not so crowded, and it also saved constant reaching for different tools. One can speak of a "combination tool" here, even if in a very original way. The experienced Lichtenfels Trade School teacher Friedrich Orlishausen always said it was not so much a question of a great number of tools as of how versatile a use of them the basket maker knew how to make.

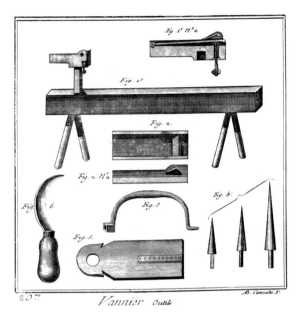

33. Weaving tools: planing bench for willow skeins, awls and other tools, copperplate from the Diderot-d'Alambert Encyclopedia.

Along with the universaly used tools, the various branches of weaving have also used tools of their own that are not known in other trades. Their numbers, as one might suspect, are not small. For example, the bowl makers had similar tools to the full willow workers, but they were individually formed and forged, such as the rapping irons, that had to be shaped differently because the bowl maker weaves thickly under the foot and can only reach and lightly strike the full willows with the front edge of the rapping iron. The hewing knives with which in olden times brown willow splints were removed and billets split resembled those of other hand-splint makers just as little. The three-legged "Hockerchen" of the bowl makers, only about seven cm high, are also unique.

It is true of all the basket maker's tools that they must fit the hand well, must not be too big, thick or rough, nor too thin and fragile, so as not to tire the user. Versatility is desired. A screwing tool handle must not cause the hand pain under heavy use, slide in the hand etc.

33

It is also very important for the basket maker to have his tools lying on the work bench, always ready to be picked up and used. The work benches newly developed at the Lichtenfels Trade School allow one to reach quickly into the interior of the bench by pulling out the movable section, without having to stand up from one's work.

Full willow work is usually done on the work board. This stands on a buck near the weaver, inclined downward away from him, so that the front edge lies on the floor. There were and are various types of work benches and boards, including those in which bench and board form a full unity in the manner of a gondola. For willow skein work a work table is needed, which must often provide space for several persons. for that reason the square work tables at the basket weaving school, with grooves for the stakes of the larger types of wood, were later fitted with drawers, which are made in rotary form because of the large numbers of students of fine work. The screwstocks for fine willow skein work too, that can be put on not freely but only over wooden forms because of the softening of the skeins, had to be designed and developed according to the handiness of the screw grips, the bracing ability of the feet, and their mobility in many directions. The wooden forms or models, called "the form" when taken as a whole, have numerous shapes, sizes, details and ways of being made. There are demountable and non-demountable ones. Sallow wood has proved to be best for them, since it, as a water-carrying plant, stands up under constant wetness as does the alder but is lighter. The carrying basket makers of the South Tirol use form boards of varying sizes, which define the form of the basket and keep it in proportion. Everything else, except the bottom board of cloven birchwood, is created as freehand weaving, measured by the eye.

The basket maker's planing bench is an important utensil in willow skein work. Along with its four legs set into holes, it bears on its long seat board two posts, usually made of pear wood and tapped and wedged into the board, between which the plane blades, with their long tongues set into grooves, are placed and attached. The wider post holds the ten pairs of slimmers in its head, the narrower one, on the left, sometimes also has a divider or ripper set into it, which halves wide skeins for the sake of thrift. The attachment of the simple pairs of slimming irons is a process that the old smiths took with them to their graves, because no one took this work seriously any more. Formerly the weavers sat in a saddle on the plane. Later the side seat was developed, which has been retained to this day. The planing benches were also subjected to revision at the school, insofar as it was possible. Uncramped seating and saving of working energy are likewise goals of all attempts to make improvements.

In palm-leaf work a wooden sulphur box is needed for preparing the fronds; its hinges must also be of wood, because the sulphurous steam arising from the sulphuring and bleaching processes attack stone and metal strongly. Besides a small knife and shears, the palm-leaf worker needs various rippers to divide the wide palm-leaf frond into equal strands of desired width. The tools are very simple and often truly brilliant inventions. The table screw for making the smallest baskets is a high right-angled block in longish quadrant form. It is wedged onto the table edge by its plate and has holes in which to put the steel spindles for the small wooden form.

The making of splint baskets particularly requires a carving bench, a cutting sawhorse, with a two-handled drawknife, also called a "fox knife", to smooth the splints and cut down the fillets for carrying baskets. All of these carving benches with varying and yet related names can be found in all of Europe.

For making basket furniture the work bench has to be big, heavily built, and mounted on strong, massive legs that are screwed fast to the workshop floor. Along with it goes a big parallel vise with soft jaws that can span the chair tube for burning. A Bunsen burner with gas line is taken for granted. The fact that many other tools are needed in basket furniture or construction weaving is a result of the fact that a variety of carpentry work has to be done. It includes whatever is needed for sawing, hole-boring, screwing, hammering and compacting.

For construction, framing and decorative weaving the same requirements for tools, apparatus and machines apply as in the other branches of weaving work that we already know.

Machines Used in Basket Weaving

For the preparation of rattan large machines are needed; they must be inmmovably attached to the floor. That is true both of peeled products and of rattan production. It has recently become customary to make basket furniture of strong formative tubes with only the glassy skin layer removed, in order to color them uniformly and keep them in even cross section. Because of their high silicic acid content, permeating all the wood in crystal form, specially hardened steel, such as Widia steel, is needed for the knives of very varied form. Thus in a chair tube factory locksmiths and toolmakers must always be on hand, less for removing actual machine waste than to sharpen the quickly dulling knives in place at short notice or to make new ones. The rattan stake is pushed into the machine and against the knife so that it comes out the other end of the machine in finished or half-finished form. The willow tree machines are farming or forestry apparatus, such as ground mills that are made to rid the ground of weeds and loosen it up between the rows of willow shoots, or planting and cutting machines for willow harvesting. Scaling machines of various sorts have been developed. Albin Reemtsma, a very capable organizer, invented a whole line of machines for willow cultivation.

At the Lichtenfels Trade School too, willow splitting, planing and slimming machines have been developed and created by capable personnel and experienced willow preparation machine makers. The master locksmith Arno Fischer of Michelau was of great service. To make simple round baskets of cheap splints a type of half-mechanical formation of the round weaving by weaving machines was created. But since a considerable amount of handwork still remained in terms of the type of weaving, delicacy and variation of form, the attempt was soon given up. Whoever has had the task of describing the production of the simplest flat plates, simple to make and without a special border, so that even an untrained newcomer can weave them, knows what is needed in procedures, numberings, movements, cuttings and measurings, beginnings and endings, settings and bendings, and knows that weaving machines would be too elaborate and costly. The course of the skein across the weave to the shape of the basket was already indicated.

The Working Processes of Basket Making

If one were to ask an individual basket maker without special training, let's say a half-farmer from the country, making splint baskets, about his work processes, if he were talkative and capable enough, he would recount a whole series of procedures used on his types of wares, or perhaps prefer to demonstrate them. The total of the work processes—not merely the binding, weaving and building types—is not very great for the individual basket maker, but wide enough in the whole range of knowledge, ability and inventiveness that he needs. Good, fully trained basket makers, on the other hand, have a great number of procedures to master. If one considers the work processes for all native and foreign basket making, then just for Central European weaving countless and varied operations appear, defined by the kind of material, application, construction, weave and binding. One of these procedures will always have advantages, and also disadvantages, compared with another. The procedure that is least problematic, that shows at once the greatest success in terms of speed, neatness, quality and beauty of work, is to be chosen. Here are a few examples of work processes to finish certain tasks with their goals, solutions and means.

We know twisted roll work only as spiral work. The spiral begins in the middle of the bottom to be made, unsupported, and usually somewhat thinner than in the following spirals. Then it runs onward in constant thickness, until upon reaching the desired size of the object it stops as abruptly as it began. On the other hand, the closed round rolls stand as if forming a bowl, all lying exactly horizontal, each one complete and separate in itself, attached to the preceding or following round with ties of string. Thus far it is a seemingly smooth thing from foot to rim, without disturbing irregularities. But every round must be closed to form a ring in the most varied ways, through many individual operations, for example, through sharming (trimming on both sides), simple setting of the two ends, or simply stuffing the ends of the straw rolls into each other. Whoever is familiar with the roll work of many lands and peoples in the folk tradition knows that this very orderly theoretical process of closed rings is found very rarely. It is a stranger to reality.

Today large stake-and-weaver work, such as laundry baskets, fruit, vegetable and potato baskets of green, white or buff full willows, is struck tight with the rapping iron. Before World War I the rapping wood was still used in the Bamberg area; with it wood struck against wood, oak or ash against willow, more protectively than striking with the iron against softened willow rods. The forged or later cast iron rapping tool has more power through its construction and the inherent weight of the steel; the materials struck by it lie better. But which of the two processes is really better, apart from the work time or expenditure of energy, for the endurance and goodness of the finished basket? Every basket can theoretically be produced in two ways: it can be made completely freehand, according to the feel of the curve, the measurement of the eye and the sight of the form. But it can also be made in many ways through models of its girth or stake form, through loose helping racks or, in the case of smaller pieces, through the use of complete forms. The wooden form is well suited to "struck" work for the achievement of exact duplications that agree in size and proportion according to the catalog.

But striking tightly together is only half the story of form in weaving. The bending of a chair tube can be done with a flame, allowing the strong stakes to be bent into not too tight half-circles. Another process might also be used: one could soften the stakes in hot water. But it would take too long until the stake was softened, then put under tension after bending, and finally so dried out that it would no longer straighten. But bending through warming with a gas flame seems to be something very new. But the ancient Bavarian ring fences were made by heating the spruce boughs for the rings on an open fire and then plaiting them into rings. Yet a kerosene lamp would burn the surface of the tube too soon, before the warmth had slowly penetrated into the interior. Electric heating has also proved not to work.

So there are many possible procedures that must be considered and chosen from.

The so-called order or sequence in the octagonal weaves of chair cane weaving is the subject of a certain mathematical process. One can begin in a great variety of ways and continue in the directions of the octagonal weave so as to draw out the actual weaving (known as "sticking") against the open spaces in a time-consuming way. In the taking of hand-drawn splints so many procedures are possible on any one tree, and even more in the case of a variety of trees, that one could create a science of it, stretching from the choice of a tree to the finished pieces, without even considering the many forms and methods or the sizes and shapes of the splint baskets. The question of whole or partial work in the handworking ways of basket making is also worth serious consideration. When elsewhere partial work is almost always regarded as an economical solution because of the involvement of the individual worker or the machine, still the question remains of whether partial work or the complete finishing of the whole piece is more advantageous, even in large series. For the preparation of the original model the complete beginning-to-end job by the model builder goes without saying. Piecework can be necessary for a very simple and serious reason, for example, if piece workers can only carry out certain processes, such as simple randing over one, under one, while the feet, transitions, borders etc. can only be done by trained personnel. Among splint basket makers piecework is necessary in a very different sense: not in dividing the work on one basket among several persons, but among several periods of time, when the rather wide weaving splints are woven wet and shrink in drying, so that the weaver first weaves a few wet rounds, lets them dry, then presses the rounds, which have shrunk somewhat away from each other, together and weaves the next few rounds. The processes of basket weaving are so vast and so many-sided that they can be presented here only fleetingly and in modest quantities.

Building, Binding, Equipping

Even before work begins, the picture of the finished piece must stand before the basket weaver's eyes, clear in its complete form and practically clear in its details. The weaving combination of all the parts into the whole work must be in one smooth flow, the unity of mass and proportion, of weaving and binding, material and application must be all-inclusive. As much as simplification, rationalization, mechanization, automation and motorization are often necessary and unavoidable in the fight for our daily bread, just as much must it be proved that basket goods and wire works not made by weaving contradict and are hostile to the concept of the woven unity.

Completely staked work: the so-called "drawn" work forms an initial picture of absolutely unified construction. By it one means a weaving work of willow tops, mostly soaked, steel-hard and at the same time flexible willows, in which absolutely no weaving out of the upsetters, no randing, wrapping or drawing out takes place, in which the stakes, likewise the stake borders, are crossed and plaited under themselves. Completely staked work has no separate, independent, completely set-off bottom, no body set upon it, and no added edge. Here in the literal sense exists a unity of material of the same kind, size and use. This work is to some extent a knot made of several strands of three to eight willows, completely identical and identically carried through and woven. It begins with the laying and weaving of, for example, six two-willow strands, and after their first attachment in bows they are brought back to the inner pivotal point of the six, usually woven over and under one strand, but also done with greater stroke lengths. This way of working, as simple and limited as it may seem, can be varied in many ways, particularly in terms of numbers, by one who knows all the means of weaving, without having to disturb the essence of the weaving requirements. In a half-staked bowl a very ordinary opened-out bottom is first woven of willow tops and sticks, into which finally the long thin willow tops are inserted as stakes. Out of this the bowed weaving and drawing together then proceeds. The ends of the willows are then brought back and woven together into a kind of foot. The construction is pieced together, but its unity was thought out in advance. The interruption through a specialized bottom formation with added bye-stakes is required by the shortness of the fine, thin, and yet conical willow tops.

Fine willow skein work gives results that are at once valuable, costly, firm and fine, light and durable. The stakes of such baskets must be measured for length in advance, and for small baskets the equally wide skeins must also be long enough to insure that the edge can either be wrapped or turned back into itself as a rich bow rim. The wrapped border, if planned and made correctly, is formed by bending the stakes, which are still standing upright, over the edge hoop, laying them horizontally along this hoop or the several hoops or edge fillets, and binding them in with the wrapping. So it cannot happen, as is often the case with very nice-looking foreign bowls, that with even a very small load in the bottom the border loosens from the stumpy cut-off stakes and cannot be reattached. In good work the question of the border must be answered already when the bottom cross or any other beginning of the bottom is commenced. Bottom cross to bottom, transition, foot, body, weave closing and border must form a unity. Significant works of basket weaving art have been completed by such building methods in a way that inspires admiration for the masterly artistic command of the weaving processes.

Unity in a Splint Basket, especially a Back Carrying Basket: generally, if not always, carrying baskets show an inner unity of stakes, corner stakes, hoops and legs with the load-carrying basket itself, which is held over the shoulders by carrying belts or other aids. If we watch such a basket coming into being, we recognize that real purpose, necessity, inner pictoriality and the power of imagination of spatial art without transitory styles have been at work here.

178–190 It is easy to see in basket furniture of any age and origin which building types and connections of the whole and the individual parts are possible and have been applied: straightline, stake-type furniture without a thick weave, in 188–190 which the seat and back surfaces are "staved", or made of closely placed stakes that provide a fairly comfortable seat with or without the help of covers or cushions. The whole thing looks light and best represents the concept of 181– furniture ("Moebel", from the Latin "mobilis", movable). Flat-surface furniture has seat planes, arms, backs, skirt or apron thickly woven, so that everything consists of flat surfaces whose connections are formed by the stakes. Spacious basket furniture was already known to the Romans. It appeared again around the turn of the century, at the time of the Youth Style, as double-walled so-called club chairs, with comfortably formed shell seats. Their 184– woven surfaces are not separated by stakes, but flow into each other and only let one suspect the presence of the stakes that carry them. Behind their spaciousness the necessary framework of leg stakes, rails, crossbars and bucks is still hiding. Mixtures and combinations of line, flat surface and block come to these clear conceptions in a constant change of furniture styles.

The question of forming space, so meaningful to the nature of basket weaving, can be seen clearly in two areas of splint basket making: the back basket begins its 86 existence as just a flat surface. The bowl, though, on account of the hoop's shape, takes form at once in its three-dimensional shape, a kind of hemisphere in many 187 variations.

The Woven Bindings

Opposed to the theoretically and practically endless weave that can extend out on all sides, the binding is the limiting as well as the limited, the closing-off, the holding-together and building-together. For example, there is a basket basin for fine baked goods, thin as suits the delicate contents. The bottom remains as a flat weave, bends upward into space without any special indication into a flat basin form, and ends in an edge. You might call it a head-footer. Here is the bottom cross that disappeared in the weaving process, here are bottom, foot, body, top rounds and border as a unity without difference, except

that the weave thickens a bit at the border. Everything is contained in one piece, and the individual, such as the foot, is transferred as a unit into the whole, even submerged in it.

On the other hand, the weave in a waste paper basket, for example, is upsett with two or three willows. Toward the edge, toward the upper end of the weave, the multiple willows are separated; instead of one willow three times, as we now have, it was formerly three willows one time. The group, the strand of three willows is spaced and divided, and the same simple randing weave, instead of going over three stakes at a time in three times the distance, now goes over and under one stake in a stroke of lesser span. That is a transition of the weave, a change limiting the height of each round, while the body weave remains the same until shortly below the rim. Through the separation of the triple weave into the simple weave, something else that is objectively necessary takes place. Because of the use of a simple weave, it becomes easy to add on the border. Through the diminishing of the distances it becomes tenser and thereby firmer. Such transitional forms, that exist in many types and groups, often change the face of the weave significantly. Here one can clearly see the change from simple weave to multiple weave, aside from the fact that the arched line formation of the stakes at the transition brings life to the strict regularity of the body-weave order.

Bottom Types and Beginnings: bottoms of baskets are generally flat. If the bottom bends upward, as a flat cone or a rounded curvature, toward the bottom it is impenetrable. The surface form of the bottom can have many facets, but it must never approach the scallops and curves of metallic or porcelain shapes. That only causes problems. The very customary natural bottom shape of the rectangle, 86 or even the square, that then changes into a circular or basket-round form in the border hoop, involves a spatial transition. It requires that very wide weaving materials, or their directions, adapt themselves to a circle with great difficulty and with many anglings of the bottom sticks. That the border hoop is round is embodied in the name "hoop", the bent and closed.

The wood bottom is the simplest form of basket base. It can be very good, for example, in the South Tirolean type of cloven birch-wood board, very tough and smoothed by hand, with holes bored in it through which the stakes are drawn and can then be fastened through various types of weaving. In the Ziller Valley fine thin spruce twigs with their bunches of needles are used, so that it is not possible to pull the stakes up out of the holes, and also so that the work goes on faster. On the other hand, cut wood bottoms to which the ribs are simply nailed can be consigned to the realm of low-value work.

114
116   The opened-out bottom, as can be concluded from successful excavations, is after the Roman board bottom the oldest base known in Europe. It can be very versatile and varied, cheap or expensive, simple or rich, loose or firm in construction, and can assume a great many shapes, allowed by changing application of weaving materials. As has been noted, the bottom must derive from the whole of the basket, defining but also defined from the start. Shape and purpose are linked to each other. The link between binding technique and appearance is of great importance in modest examples as well as in large pieces.

The techniques, variations, degrees of firmness, bye-staking, form, materials, the question of whether to begin with the butt or top end of the willow when weaving, when laying the willow in, and a thousand other things make the question of the simple, straightforward, uninvolved opened-out bottom so vast in scope.

Just the question of the needle-and-thread position, whether the bottom cross is to be formed simply by laying the two crossing sticks (several of each) over each other or by splitting one set and sticking the others through them at right angles, is not only to be thought about, but has a lot to do with formation and may well lead to different bottom shapes and forms.

The stock base, well known from the laundry baskets with rectangular bottom shape, can be regarded as the simplest bottom. It consists of long base sticks for which good willow stakes were chosen, and of a simple randed weave of white full willows. For the bottom sticks nowadays one likes to use flat-elliptical softwood fillets cut by machine.

Beyond that, the simplest of bases can take many forms in the hands of one who has a wide mastery of the inherent weaving possibilities and does not cling too strictly to habit and the habitual.

152–157   This type of bottom is, moreover, not different from the oldest type of construction of vertical house walls and fences made of stakes driven vertically into the ground with horizontal weaving (randing), which has lasted from ancient times into our own century (for example, in Rumania).

113   The Star Bottom: the simplest known straw stars, in which a group of straws of equal length are laid on each other and separated in the form of a star, are also the basic concept for the woven star bottom. But since all the stakes or straws cross each other in the middle, if one used willow stakes for it, there would be an extraordinary thickening in the middle, which would be unbearable for a basket bottom. So the star bottom is limited in that it allows wide stakes, to be sure, but only very thin ones. Very thin willow skeins, thin year-old wood splints, flattened rushes, cattail leaves, and in particular palm leaves and the finest bamboo skeins form the basis of the star bottom, can be bound and woven, bye-staked and sometimes also staved, that is, woven lightly, with spaces, in many ways. The star bottom can be round or basket-round (a rounded rectangle). Other forms, such as the square or rectangle, are also possible.

The procedures of bye-staking are varied and closely 162 linked to the components of multiple weaving, likewise with cutting of stakes standing too close, picking, when the belly of the basket, for example, narrows into a neck.

The bound bottom is particularly necessary when strong stakes, not windable at the prevailing distance 347 between stakes, are to continue from bottom to border 400 and cannot be woven against each other in two directions. 324 One direction is laid, the second, longer or shorter, crosses it at right angles, and both are bound together with windable skeins or strings. Thus patterns like cross-stitching can be formed with the strokes that cross each other at acute and right angles, so that the necessity of binding works together with decorating; that is always the most pleasant form of blending technique and shaping, so that both are fulfilled. Squares and rectangles can be formed, and if necessary the two directions can also cross at acute instead of right angles.

In the laid bottom all kinds of light or heavy skein 365 weaves can be used. The weave is begun when the stakes in one direction are attached to the wooden form with the help of nail fillets, at the right distance from each other, at one end of the planned bottom square or rectangle, and then those in the other direction or directions are woven in. This type of work is as customary in Upper Franconia as in China or Japan, especially when the border is then fastened with hoops or fillets, bound to the stakes and then wrapped.

The high and deep bottom is related to the bound bottom in that the stakes that pass from the border to the 86 body and base and reach up to the other side of the rim are 399 not windable and therefore are bound together with thin willows or willow skeins that are woven between the stiff stakes. The weave is very three-dimensional, strong, and makes striking shadow effects. One sometimes calls it the Japanese high and deep bottom. If one had looked at native splint baskets, especially the bottoms of carrying baskets, the "Japanese" designation surely would not have come into being.

The staved bottom is used chiefly in France; it is very airy, light and friendly. When it is staked closely, it also requires a special fastening of the body stakes to the bottom sticks. They are held between fitches standing very far apart. The total weight of a basket is made especially light thereby. It can also be done with two willows and varied in other ways.

39

The light spiral bottom belongs to a group of spiral roll work types. It has long been known in Michelau, and it was done in olden times with full willow inlays and willow skeins as socalled "pierced work", later with round rattan and willow skeins. All kinds of geometrical weaving patterns can be created with it, not unlike cross-stitching or the bound and tied weaves and bottoms.

The knot bottom, which is known throughout the world, is also a kind of drawn bottom, in which knot shapes are made out of one or more strands of single full willows, willow tops, etc., in many variations. The weaving art of the Far East has accomplished a particular lot in this area. It is a matter of flat knots that are not completely tied but left lightly tied.

The pretzel knot, actually the simplest knot that exists, can be plaited and drawn together in multiple ways, as well as with multiple willows. The binding knots of spiral roll work belong in this category too, and the concept of bottom types in basket weaving in general could be expanded considerably. (Inspiration can be found in, among others, the systematizing of knots by Dr. Johannes Lehmann.)

The foot formations are just as numerous as the other groups of binding. There are baskets, such as ladies' purses for the theater, that need no foot. Other footless types are hung on the wall or come in utensils where they rest safely and can be switched. A third type doesn't need one because their bottoms are woven flat or even slightly crowned upward. All types of feet provide not only good standing but, above all, also protection of the weave against loosening. One need only look at the foot formation of back baskets. A brief mention of the individual foot names and designations may indicate how basket weaving has developed: there are the footless flat bottom, the crowned footless bottom, the napped, pointed or knobbed foot, the rimmed foot, the fillet or hoop foot, the bye-staked and partly woven foot, the foot and body going on as a unit, the woven-in stake foot, the stake foot inserted from below, the foot bound on from outside, the mortised corner stakes, the sharp fillet foot and still others, all in variable form and construction.

Basket borders: here we know the borderless basket, that is, the basket in which the stakes end without any binding, also the stakes that are stuck back in, usually broad, thin upsetters that are bent over the hoop and inserted into the weave, for example in birch bark, palm- leaf work etc., also open borders, in which the round or flat thin stakes are stuck into the weave to the side in arched form. Stake-woven borders have a simple closing of the weave or one bound with fillets, of which there are many types, wherein the stake ends are bent to the left or right and plaited into each other. The simplest type is the

34. Clamps made of forked branches, to help hold border hoops before the final binding, still used in Upper Austria and the Bavarian Woods.

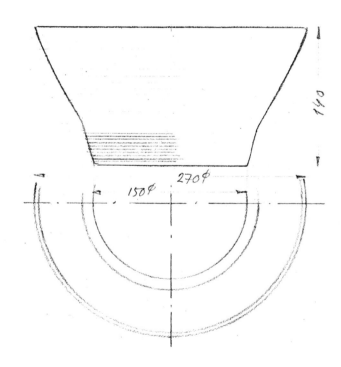

35. Simple, very small-scale working drawing (pattern drawing) for a Mitwitz palm-leaf basket of any desired size.

"Kipprand" (rolled border), in which the stake is laid over or under one or more stakes at once and then cut off. The fastening or limiting takes place simply, in that the stake is held where it comes out of the closed weave, wound over the next stakes, and so fixed by friction. In spite of the simple process and the very limited number of strokes, indeed only a half-stroke, hundreds of variations on the rolled border can be formed by other means, such as stroke length (number of over- and underbound nearby stakes), multiple willow work of various origins, dividing of multiple willows, etc.

The trac border (Einschlag) is a continuation in which a whole stroke, two halves, or more strokes, any number one wants, can be applied. From this, even when one thriftily goes only up to four strokes, it is easy to see that many more, even hundreds of border patterns can result. It has been said that not only does the number of strokes increase considerably, but so does the number of other weaving processes.

While the rolled and trac borders are simple, and every stake is finished in order in various successions of strokes, so that it is not disturbed or touched again until the ends are cut off and trimmed, making a plain border (Zuschlag) of a row of stakes is harder, as its beginning, its introduction, is richer and thus more formative, more variable. The individual stakes are not taken once, but twice, and sometimes more times, not laid at once in a whole preplanned series of strokes, but only for the first time, after which the following stakes are laid the first time, then one returns to the first stake and lays it completely. It goes, so to speak, two steps forward and one back.

One can observe the plain border well on potato baskets, laundry baskets and the like. It is thick, does not stick out like the beloved, decorative braided border, in danger of being cracked, but lies tightly on the closing of the weave.

The braided border is really a plaiting of the stake ends with each other, while the rolled, trac and plain borders are only a kind of crossing.

The "Wurstelrand" (sausage border!) is a variant of the staked border that has spread all over Europe; in the Federal Republic it is still found in the area of Kulmbach and the Plassenburg, between the Frankenwald and Franconian Alb, and especially in the Margraves' and Hohenzollern lands.

The aforementioned drawn border is basically nothing more than a plaited trac border, usually of multiple willows, in which the stakes are, however, not drawn and struck close together, but remain separate and light. In the last decades, in fact since about 1918, it has fallen very much out of use because of the increasing simplification of weaving.

Other borders include, for example, the bound border, which looks best in splint weaving, the wrapped border, of which the Lichtenfels Trade School alone has produced some five hundred patterns through students' experiments and competitions, and which can be expanded considerably according to one's knowledge of the ways of weaving and all its main types, can almost approach textile weaving through its fineness, and can definitely attain the latter's ornamental variety (colorful woven bands). Wrapping, overwrapping, two-tone pairing, edging and plaiting are the main methods, which can also be used (as in India) for closing spiral work in quite fine strips of palm leaf.

The mixed borders, for example among stake borders alone, among the wrapped borders with fillets or multiple hoops, present an apparently unlimited variety. But the building of the object, its purpose, and above all a sensible formation show how to avoid a mixture of border types if they do not provide needed firmness. The excellence with which, for example, the old Michelau basket weavers bordered their fine works, the beautiful agreement with the whole, can still set an example of disciplined work.

The wooden bindings of basket furniture are in a new growth. The work of framing is also the work of shaping. But this begins with the handworked bindings, the plaited bindings. Only now, once again, are bindings really appropriate to wood applied, which were developed in the Fifties at the basket weaving school. These bindings, including doubling and the old triangle bindings, are thus not simple matters as in the formation of basket furniture, because unlike hardwood and steel tube furniture, the palm-tube stakes flex too easily. So firmness and simplicity can be achieved less through legs, braces and weaves than through bucks and crossbars, struts and strengthenings.

The equipping of basket wares with lids, handles, handholds etc. is both a necessity for use and an adornment. The spacious, massive-looking basket, closed by a lid, takes on a more easygoing appearance through leg sticks and handles and the like, as these are naturally a necessity in a very obvious sense. There are also many kinds of lids. There are those that fall on, over and in; their forming and bottom building must usually be like, or similar to, the basket bottoms; their height measurements are determined by their purpose or use; so a sewing basket lid can serve as both a work surface and an upholstered sewing cushion. The knobs or rings that carry the basket or lid are just as varied in form. Short rounded knobs break the spatial fulness of the whole basket. The handles with their thin hoop lines likewise make it look freer and lighter. Handholds and fixed or movable rings make use easier just as they ease the impression of massiveness in a

41

complete closed work or sewing basket. The handes form a considerable realm of shaping in their arrangement, size, attachment, form, movement, and ways of being made and wrapped.

300 The closing apparatus too, the noose, the hasp and the latch pegs once so gracefully formed and hung on willow skein chains, are enriching and enlivening additions to the uniform woven surface of the basket, created once again out of necessity and deliberate form. The partitions of the 359–364 baskets make the inner picture livelier. The peasant weaving styles, as also those old Upper Franconian or the new classically fine ones, likewise show a combination of necessity and beauty in their woven interior divisions.

240–246 Additional equipment is found in the form of the belt or carrying straps and other carrying aids, which even in 250–252 back baskets are a little world in themselves, especially when one sees them gathered from all over the world. They include braids, chains, strings, cords and woven bands (of rushes, straw or cattails). They should be made either by weaving of weaving materials or out of other natural materials, such as raw leather, linen or cotton cloth, such as can also be used to line the interiors of baskets. Plastic sheets have also proved useful for hand baskets with or without lids, but with their shining glossiness they form no living union with the natural weaves.

The Bindings of Frame Weaving: the wooden frames of many types of furniture, also of bedsteads, must be wide, for the tube weave for them is usually under strong tension, like that of piano wires, and too small and thin frames would be pulled in by it. The thickness of the frame is determined by the kind of boring, which cannot go completely through, in order to leave the back or inside of the furniture smooth and undisturbed. The socalled Viennese boring, which also leaves the back of the frame unbroken, is very demanding and therefore is not usually used. The oldest type, with holes bored completely through, is likewise avoided, despite its useful simplicity, because the backs of the frames are rough and catch dust with the knots of the tube bands. Pegging with wooden pegs, which are driven into the bored holes along with the ends of the woven bands and glued there, has proved to be best. When the inner upper folded corners of the frames are rounded off, the highly tense weave cannot shear off and thus lasts much longer. Single bands can at times be woven out, that is, drawn along. Usually, though, the whole weave would have to be opened and drawn in all over again to repair damage caused by use, because one had waited too long with the repairs.

The bindings of building and decorating weaves resemble those of the other branches of weaving work. Yet it is allowed and practiced, for example in decorative weaving, to make ornamental use of bindings, such as letting evenly cut and ordered stake ends stand as a sort of fringe. Since this work is not usually applied to frequently used utilitarian baskets, the work can be done more loosely, attractively and decoratively.

Examples of Binding Variations

The ways of weaving can be applied in binding in just as rich variety as in the weave itself. As there, the variation of bindings, structures and forms is a question of the inventive gift. The knowledge of weaving direction, stroke length and number, number of weavers, change of stroke and its direction, ways of weaving, over- and under-binding, attachment, division etc., is most useful in making a little world of bindings arise with the help of varied numbers. The lower numbers are especially effective therein. The term and concept of "original numbers" were proclaimed and developed by Hugo Kluegelhaus. The use of the lower numbers in basket weaving is obvious, even if nothing has yet been written about it. Dividing by even and odd numbers, for example, is of such significance with three-strand plaited triple 268 weave that even-numbered stakes, as opposed to odd numbers, give a completely different weaving pattern when all the other conditions are the same. Border areas and relationships to mathematics and mathetics (Wilhelm Ostwald: the science of order) should be mentioned here.

The simple opened-out bottom is not at all to be taken as lightly here in terms of weaving beginnings as its appearance makes one think. On the bottom the crossing of several axial sticks is made in cruciform. The number of sticks can vary from one to about eight in each direction, that reach from the bottom cross of a round basket to the longest part of the basket circle. The number of sticks in each direction can be even or odd. That allows any combination of numbers, but depends on the size of the bottom, the thickness of the stakes and the purpose of the basket. The length of the cross sticks, their numbers, especially in the relation of the needles to the threads, can be varied and depends on the final distance between stakes in the basket weave and the number of weavers to be woven in. In these simple bottoms many characteristics are found that are variable in themselves and can also be varied in relation to their surroundings and neighbor-hoods. The slath, that actually holds the bottom cross together, the opening-out area and finally the actual weave that usually continues uniformly to the edge of the bottom, can each be woven in a single round, but also in several rounds, carried out two or three times with constant or changing numbers. The rounds can increase outwardly, can lessen or change in goodly quantities.

Types of weaving in the slath, opening-out and uniformly woven areas can be varied easily for different effects. The actual bottom weave can be randed, layered, twilled, fitched or waled, it can be light or heavy.

The staked borders depend on a plentitude of weaving processes with rich use of weaving means and numbers. In staked border weaving it is first of all a matter of a row of numbered stakes from which as much as possible must be derived. One will not stop with simple counting, but make use of singular and plural, even and odd, counting forwards and going backwards (see the plain border!), dividing and combining, etc.

In a single-willow row of stakes each stake stands alone by itself, each separated from the others by regular and always equally great distances, which cannot differ in the piece independently of others. We can count the stakes in twos, threes or fours, can divide them evenly or unevenly, weave them to two or more stakes in plaiting the border. Thereby the plaiting of stakes that from the start are set up by twos forms a different picture than a border in which the two-willow work only begins with the making of the border. The numerical order can also be set up with varying numbers, in that some are doubled and others single. The variation is a very enriching and also startling means of weaving. With it the weave becomes richer, the pattern, rapport and repetition longer and more inclusive.

The Weave in Shape Formation: the transition from the actual body weave to the body frame, as in a carrying basket, is not always easy to determine. If a carrying basket has one or two wide splints built in at the front, where the carrying belts are to be fastened, to strengthen the weave and the whole part of the basket, then these must be woven over. Then this part of the basket appears to be a whole weave, varied with wide and narrow stakes or ribs. This leads to the inspiration to make use of a rhythmic variation of wide and narrow stakes in other baskets and to consider this in building them.

In the complete construction, not in flat panels of weaving models but in arched basket or round bottom, whose stakes run out in star shape and finally become too far apart, the job of bye-staking can be understood as one limited by the technique of the handicraft and yet a freely variable shaping weave. Here one might think of the Emsdetten grain bowls of Roman origin or the shell seats of basket furniture.

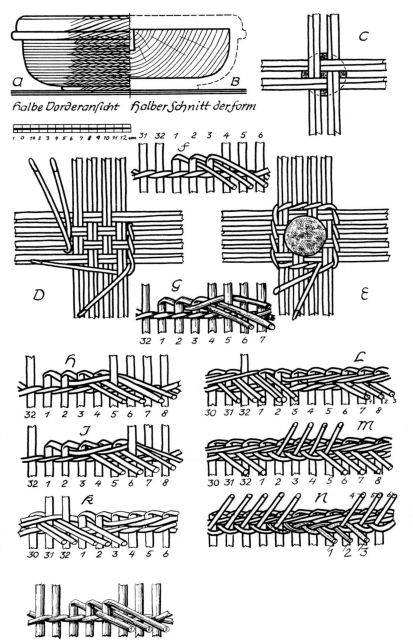

36. Upper left: the weave; right: cut through the wooden form. Below: examples of rush weaving processes (bottom and border).

43

Types of Weaving and their Methods

The question of how many types and patterns of weaving there might be in the world cannot be answered. But the question of how many weaves (not the spatial application of the weaves in the most varied basket forms and ways of building them) a simple splint basket maker ought to have at his command is simple to answer. There are two or three. A capable Upper Franconian fine basket maker, though, has in mind so many major ways of weaving and their variations that he has woven, invented or adapted in his work that it is not easy to bring them all together. A weaving teacher at the Lichtenfels Trade School once asked how many different types of weave (patterns) could be used in a "limited" weave—with definite limits in number and means. The following means were codified:

1. With one type of material: poplar.
2. Only one means of use: peeled veneer splints.
3. Only one cross-section form: thin, narrow, right-angled.
4. Only one measurement: 10 to ½ mm (thus not thick stakes and thin weavers).
5. Only one color: bright natural color.
6. Only one means of binding: crossing.
7. Only two to eight directions.
8. Only stroke lengths over and under 1 to 8.
9. Only changes of stroke from 1 to 6.
10. Change direction (in twill etc.) from the left and from the right.
11. Only one skein situation: constantly flat.
12. Number of weavers from one to four.
13. Distance between stakes: close, ½, 1/1 and 2/1 of the skein breadth.

A hasty reckoning gave about 50,000 different patterns. This number seemed faulty; one thought that repetitions or practical impossibilities must exist. A young teaching aide at the school, who had studied mathematics and combinations, found the proof of its rightness, at first even with further limitations of numbers, and mathematics professors and students at the Technical College confirmed the calculation. Without practical significance within itself, when one leaves out the combinations, permutations and variations that might well lead to the invention of additional patterns, the calculation shows how many concealed possibilities there are in the weaving art.

The Lapped Weaves: their form depends on lapping, that is, the undulation of all or a certain row of the weaving materials. Against the undulation, the bending, the weaving plant defends itself. It wants to stay straight. For that it makes pressure and counterpressure in all directions. Rubbing pressure (friction), as the name suggests, causes rubbing. This arrested rubbing of weaving ranges from the inflexible immobility of the willows to a loose flexibility. The tension of the material, defined by an original firmness and limited by the cross section, and the power of the undulation, determine the extent of the firmness. One can try this crossing oneself at various angles, not just right angles, with a few splints or thin wood fillets and see how many such splints or willows or rattan sticks suffice to make a basic weave hold without glue or nails. It does not matter if two or more directions bend or if, as in simple staked randing, the stakes remain stiff and unmoved and the weaving willows are all the more moving, bending and being made crooked against their natural will.

The hung weaves, as a firming type of binding, are still in part under the law of limiting, of friction. But since they are forerunners or followers of knitted or crocheted binding, and these hooked works are thoroughly firm in themselves—even though movable—and always hold together, here the main cause of firmness is the law of mechanics, according to which a body cannot be where another body already is. A wool yarn or rattan ribbon cannot pass through the previous or next one; it is imprisoned, and so a whole row of hung weaving is hanging from the previous one and cannot fall down. Such weaves exist in very simple as well as very rich forms.

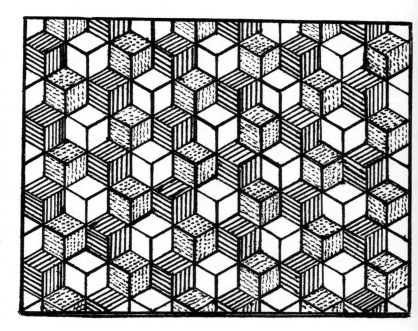

37. Schematic drawing of a tight three-colored six-pointed star weave. Example of one of the many color arrangements possible through numerical variation and pictorial conception.

40
44
45

38. *Finest Indonesian palm-leaf work in natural color, the small cigarette box (right foreground) somewhat bleached. Significant forms of decoration and examples from the East Asian islands.*

39. Handled basket of white willow skeins, ribbed high and deep weave. The stakes that stand out make the basket form especially recognizable.

40. Women's handbags of very fine willow skeins, presumably once dyed. Michelau work, circa 1830.

41. Handled basket with upsetters (ribs) of brown willow knife veneer splints, white full willow woven layers (cubes), rods with tips laid in, back-staked border, bare double splint handle.

42. Hand splint newspaper rack, stakes set in holes in the bottom board.

272 The Bound, Wrapped, Tied or Forced Weaves: this type of binding occurs most often in wrapped roll weaves.
101–103 The straw roll, for example, is bound together with the weaving strokes. This wrapping ribbon also pulls and binds the following roll to itself at a close or farther distance, and also the preceding roll, more precisely stated, to the location lying under it, for there is only one single roll, which runs in spirals from the beginning of the bottom to the closing of the border, forming itself.

The bound-up weave, in which two loose stake positions, one lying over the other, are wrapped together with winding ribbon, as also in the so-called tied weave, depends on the same mechanical law of binding. Very much like the crossed weaves, it presses two willows lying across each other close together through the binding stroke. There again friction results, and thereby fastening. In all cases binding two rolls together can also be done with space between, which is accomplished with knots, as for example in Upper Franconian palm-leaf work. In the many ways that were and are used, this knot itself can attach the wrapping and binding willows or skeins along with it. These three types of weave are the mechanically effected basic procedures of weaving binding and fastening. Interim forms and "diagonal bindings" certainly exist and can be expanded on.

The Most Important Basic Weaves from the Three Basic Weaves: the aforementioned crossing weaves can be divided further into various groups, even the most often-used basic weave type, the staked lapped weave. The most
7 common variant, the staked weave, consists of strong, stiff sticks, stakes, ribs, with winding, more flexible willows woven around them in waves of alternating under- and overbinding until the woven surface has taken form and been made firm in itself. Thus in particular the randed,
43 layered, bodied, slewed, cubed and stepped weaves of full
151 basket willow are formed. Every ancient fence was woven this way, as also the panels of half-timbered houses. The technique can be refined, not only through the use of thinner, softer, more delicate materials, but also through finer types of weaving. Variations of staked weaves are the more artistically woven-through types, such as the twisted and plaited weaves, the twisted and pressed fitches, the wales that wind not only around the stakes but also around each other. These can be refined through special skein positions, as the pressed or twisted fitches and wales are, in which again the weaving ribbon twists one or more times around itself and thereby achieves a particular firmness of weave as well as a pearly effect of the
104 individual strokes and the woven surface. One also calls
109 these fitches and wales "windings". Thus the plaited weaves, the triple and quadruple weaves are made, that once again form a very noticeable enriching and firming of the staked weave.

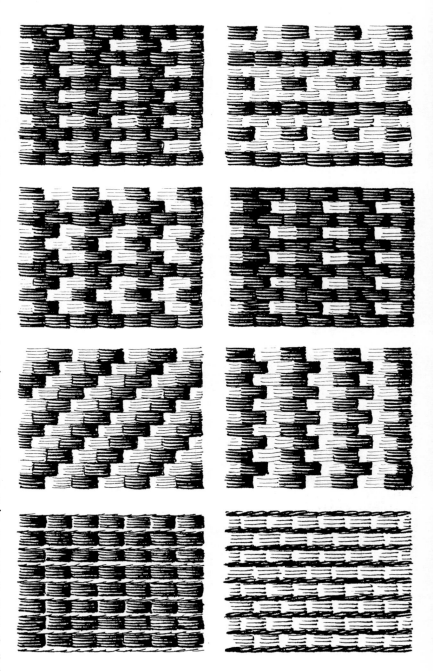

43. Examples of the variation of two-color full willow cube weave, Upper rows: Cube weaves over two stakes, cube strokes offset one stake from round to round. Lower examples: simple cube strokes over two stakes, alternating with different-colored fitched rounds. Effect of color division.

The plaited border and the plaited weaves (three- and fourply weaves) are closely related to the plait formed for its own use, as we find it in the braids of women's hair styles. Along with plaiting goes a further special type of weaving, knotting. This occurs in East Asia in the form of knotted, bound and plaited hair bands of the thinnest bamboo shoots. Diagonal bindings among the groups of basic weaves, the crossed, hung and bound, are also numerous in theory and practice. In equal crossed weaves there is no difference between stakes and randing willows. They can be built of two or more positions. Triangular,

143–146 hexagonal or octagonal weaves, like the right-angled or acute-angled crossed and randed weaves (with spaced

365 stakes), the sieve weaves (with space in both directions), and the slewed weaves (with no space either way, completely tight) generally have equally thick, though not always equally wide skeins.

136 The Dueten weaves with staking are common today. One can see them on lighting fixtures (lampshades) and women's handbags. Decades ago in the Upper Franconian area around Mitwitz they were used in weaving little Easter baskets as border decorations, were also collected, and one day were gotten out again when one wanted to create echo-breaking weaves with very rough surfaces. As construction weaving they then disappeared again, after large ones had been used in various places. One day, though, they appeared anew on lampshades and handbags.

Rare Weaves in Europe and Overseas: in the Michelau Basket Museum an old Japanese basket is preserved whose staking shows bamboo staves in almost baroque forms. For years thebasket maker had gathered particular growths, so as to be able to weave a single such basket.

Today, for example, China exports baskets made of broad bands of maize leaves knotted like cord, which show an astounding variety of weaves not yet seen among us. Indonesia has created in its palm-leaf weaving highly artistic weave types whose analysis causes even a very experienced weaver some trouble. Many weaves are created with microscopic precision and win admiration from all sides.

The Impressions of Weaves:

General Impression: quiet/lively, even/uneven, glossy /matt etc.
Fineness or coarseness in relation to the size of the basket.
Surface: smooth, rough, flexible, obstinate, flattish, angular.

Texture: very tight, thickly loose, airy, pierced, wide-mesh.
Thickness: very thin, thick, massive, leathery.
Sidedness: smooth on both sides, externally or internally rough, lively, tangled.
Shadow Effect: flat, strongly shadowed, individual shadows, stroke shadows.
Color effect: fresh, natural, artificial, not colorful. Colorful.
Sound: dull, dry, soft, fine-toned.
Atmosphere: fresh, plantlike, moldy, boring, blooming, healthy.

The Stake Interval: in weaving the distance between stakes is important. A closer stake interval is better 162 looking, firmer, more durable, nobler, more valuable and also more expensive. It requires more willows, longer work time, finer fingers and slower, costlier work. Naturally, close weaving work also allows finer types of weaving and decoration. Numbers can have many kinds of meaning and application in weaving too: width, mass, gauge or thickness, indication of multiple willows, and in the sums of many smaller numbers such as varying width, stroke length, over- and underbinding, the number of bottom sticks and their division as well as their opening out, the number of slath and opening-out directions, the number and order or weaving directions, they can be the numbers of the stakes, they can indicate the positions of colors in woven patterns etc.

The opening out of the bottom sticks is a matter of 104 measurement with the eye, of well-ordered mirror images, 114–1[but also of numbers. Here sober numbers, technical necessity and beauty form a unity from which one could subtract only at the cost of a work's quality. The purposefulness of the opening-out processes, for example whether the four stakes of a crossarm should all be opened out at once, bent away from each other in order to attain the necessary stake interval in ray form, or whether one separates the stakes from each other in pairs, two and two, or if one should leave the two middle stakes of each crossarm together, different from the rest, for firmness and bind each outer stake (bottom stick) together with the nearest stake of the next crossarm, is a matter of choice in opening out: 4 = 2 + 2 or 1 + 2 + 1, etc. These are all questions of work speed, quality, firmness and beauty; they require a deep knowledge of the weaving art if one is to answer them validly. In basket-round bottoms the question also arises of whether the long stakes in the bottom cross are chosen to be multiple and then bound together in steps. Here there is also the problem of dividing a number, for example, that of five bottom sticks. Take the 104 five lowest numbers in the ways they could be divided:

1 = 1
2 = 1 + 1
3 = 1 + 1 + 1 = 2 + 1 = 1 + 2 (2 outside or 2 inside!)
4 = 1 + 1 + 1 + 1, = 2 + 1 + 1, = 1 + 2 + 1, = 2 + 2, = 3 + 1, =
   1 + 3.
5 = 1 + 1 + 1 + 1 + 1, = 2 + 1 + 1 + 1, = 1 + 2 + 1 + 1, = 1 +
   1 + 1 + 2, = 1 + 1 + 2 + 1, = 2 + 2 + 1, = 2 + 1 + 2, = 1 +
   2 + 2, = 2 + 3, = 3 + 2, = 3 + 1 + 1, = 1 + 3 + 1, = 4 + 1, =
   1 + 4

44. *Simple crossed sieve weave, which can be varied in many ways, through width, angles, number of willows and their alternation.*

These divisions of numbers are in part mirror images, in part unrelated, which in most cases is quite acceptable, for example, when in making a drawn bowl, one applies the 3 + 1 relation so that the stronger bundling with three willows comes outside and thus gives the impression of greater firmness. In the often customary illumination of a drawn bowl the unequal and thus comparatively "disorderly" appearing divisions can have a relaxing and charming effect. By repeating the inequality six times, as in a six-stroke bowl, order is brought back into the picture. The intervals can also be varied here.

What is Characteristic of a Simple Randing Weave?

One determines, for example, that the vertical willows are equal to the horizontal ones in width. From that it derives that the breadths are variable, that the weave can be woven wide and coarse, or fine, ribbon-fine, but also that the horizontal willows can be wide, the vertical ones slim, or vice versa. In the patterns shows the vertical ones are all equally wide. They can also be alternatingly wide and slim, and this alternation could likewise be 1 : 2 : 1 : 2, but also 1 : 1 : 2 : 1 : 1 : 2 etc. The vertical willows could all be the same width, the horizontal ones varying, or both directions could show variation, etc. But that is only one of the many characteristics of a simple randing weave. In reality there are hundreds of basic qualities that can be shown, varied, changed and extended. The realm of basket weaving also shows many signs of plane and solid geometry. Therefore the theory of proportion certainly belongs among the knowledge of a well-trained weaver.

Here we refer only to the geometry of hexagonal or octagonal weaving. Some has already been suggested in the randing weave. At the Lichtenfels Trade School series of experiments and variations were made on octagonal weaves with chair cane. In the firm handling of the weaving process practiced there, one ought to see that even in polygonal weaving, as in randing, only a few free, variable weaving means were available. Yet there are a number of individual figures in these weaves. Playing with the designed woven networks can lead to rich, impressive but also expensive weaves, which one can also improve with other-colored, at least darker inlays.

45. *Light, drawn-out starred hexagonal weave.*

Circle Geometry: the cross sections of the willows, the natural tubes, the rushes, reeds etc., and the machine-produced round rattans are circular, or in the case of rattan skeins, parts of a circle. The rules of working with circles are very clear and applicable to the workshop, especially in the making of basket furniture frames. Here the assembly with screws or dowels is very important in terms of the circle, of circle and circle inside and out, and of circle and straight line.

The fitch inside the stake weaving is a basic form of weaving. We already find it in the oldest ornaments from Crete and in early Greece (Archaic Era). The woven patterns on stone ornaments of the Langobards, the Arian Christians, like those of the Celts, who used circles more strictly, are shown in these pictures, along with the law of waves.

The wrapping of leg stakes in basket furniture, like that of basket and handle hoops, is also based on the laws of circle geometry. A wrapping that is not laid strictly tangentially and radially, thus in the direction of the arc radius, will slip, because only the exactly right-angled section and its contact provide the shortest distance around a cylinder.

The geometry of basket forms and proportions (cubic measures) is also very exact and alive, in whichever way the baskets and furniture are formed: freehand, with molds or over a form. In all cases a strict conception of form must precede the procedure. Whether this is done in combination with arcs or arcs with straight lines, hyperbolic or parallel forms, ellipses, in basket-round or free form is a matter of many conditions and circumstances. A basket shape can arise in freehand body-shaping, take form and develop as it is made, if the inventiveness of the weaver's hand directs the willow according to its own nature and maintains the required form. In contrast, the form of the basket's top view, the border hoop and the bottom can be made of straight lines and sections of circles. Molds can be made highly tight and appropriate to the weaving material with shears by folding and cutting. It is the freedom of the observant and critical basket weaver that he can improve the work beyond drawing and mold in weaving it.

The Ordering of Weaving Ornamentation

229–231 The stricter kind of organization consists chiefly of lining, mirroring, that is, symmetry around one, two or more 339–342 axes, the rotating around a center or pole. They all lie hidden in the simple randing weave. The tendency that pushing and twisting can make use of (Wilhelm Ostwald) constitutes another form of order or means of shaping. In the weave the orders unite in many ways: simple figures

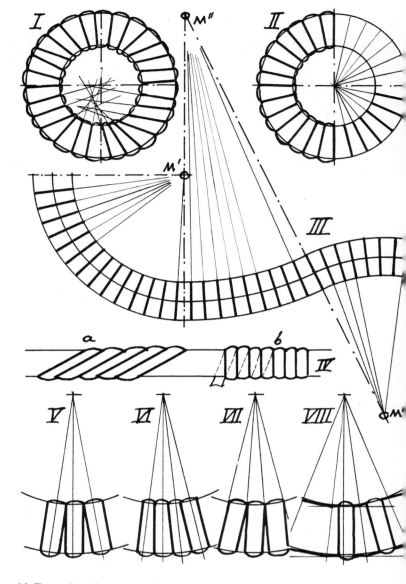

46. Examples of correct and incorrect wrapping according to the laws of circles.

mirror themselves two or four times, in three- or six-cornered weaves three or six times, rotating shapes are made out of originally unordered forms.

Diamond shapes and their variations are mainly results of the weaving strokes over and under two or more stakes. Their origins are found in the small diamonds that form without compulsion in the randed or slewed weave. That the diamonds are usually lying, with horizontal long axes, is a natural result of the stake interval in opposition to the close-lying randed rounds. Out of the full diamonds and the half-diamonds at the borders, which sometimes enclose an inner diamond, they form numerous, often very rich images as they press against and into each other. We found them particularly distinct among the straw braid pouches of the Tuscan weavers; they have also spread throughout the whole world. Numeerous variations

50

47-49. Sets of three nested baskets, from the Gagel catalog.

have arisen in Michelau. But these were not adaptations from embroidery, but decorations that derived from the essence of weaving, especially the manifold use of the stroke length and change of stroke.

For the many kinds of weaving decorations the diamonds are only an introductary example. Every genuine weaving decoration is formed through the constant repetition of the basic pattern, then goes beyond it, outshines it. Among the charming types of decoration in weaving, the following main groups stand out:

The continuing weave, in constant repetition of the basic pattern, is in all its ways and variations a decoration in itself by its bound nature. Figures and structures, forms and joints, above all smaller weaving forms and figures mix with each other as transitions.

The geometrical forms, as adaptations of the stroke length, but also composed of many other weaving means, are very varied in the different branches of the basket weaver's profession, different countries and materials in any case, and therefore can be made in limitless forms: 50 crosses, stars, meanders etc.

Simplified symbols of plants arise similarly, as children transpose and portray what they have seen in the simplest way. So we find the Thuringian fir tree or the Sardinian-Hebraic plant and flower pictures portrayed in simplified form. The Tree of Life as a Nordic or Indogermanic symbol is not rare.

The Animal Ornament: a round type of Grecian meander, the symbolization of the winding course of the Meander River, called the "Running Dog", is the most simplified, most objectively adapted portrayal of the living and animal. The meander, which can be found in Greece, Sardinia, among the Indians as well as the Chinese, follows the wave rule.

In Spain a three-dimensional steer's head, woven of white willows, is worn over the head as a child's plaything. In general, though, animal portrayals are seen considerably more rarely in weaving work than they are in embroidery.

The human being is seen in weaving as a bridal couple, man and woman, Adam and Eve, often in very fine spiral roll work. The Mexican Indians and their descendants 408 weave excellent full figures out of rushes, even riders and musicians, but also Christmas mangers, Christmas tree angels and various other items of straw. They know how to make the things very recognizable and likewise faithful to the rush forms, but without falling into the false pride of attributing a human anatomy to the rushes.

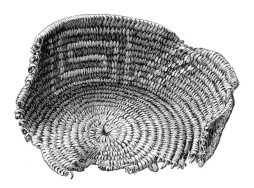

50. Fragment of very old Indian spiral weaving. The meander running to the left is very rare. In addition to America (especially Mexico) woven meanders are still found in Greece, Sardinia, China and Indonesia.

The West Upper Franconian "Doggerla" are small dolls that run as decoration in two, three or four circuits around the bodies of white willow city baskets, which are made for trips to the city. Sometimes these circuits are all alike, sometimes two are the same while the third is different. So every basket maker creates his own trade mark. There are not many types of decorative rounds that keep running like the Running Dog and finally meet each other. Today it is hard to buy the necessary fine and very finest willows in Germany.

Surface Treatment and Coloring

Raw weaving plants, even the white willows, must usually be cleaned when they have been stored a long time. Plants that have grown wild, especially those that grew along the water and stood in high water at times, such as rushes and cattails, must of course be washed, and in any case they need to be softened before use. The preparation of materials, such as smoothing or planing, must take place at the right time. Sulphuring or bleaching is likewise a part of surface treatment, as is lacquering or varnishing. But priority must be given to protection from worms and rot, especially when the plants were harvested at the wrong sap-running time. In every kind of handling, the basket weaver has to consider that the protective materials he uses, such as gloss lacquer, must not be injurious; that applies particularly to woven wares meant to carry food. Lacquers applied too thickly can look obtrusive and greasy. Milder substances such as wax should be added to common lacquers, especially nitro-lacquers, so they will look less glossy or retain a gentle sheen from light rubbing of their surface. Many foreign imports get a very mediocre coat of artificial lacquer that smells as rancid as an old coat of fat and is inferior in every way to the fine old lacquers, such as those of the Japanese. On the subject of color in the world of basket weaving, it must be clearly differentiated between what is color and what is colorful (to the extent of mixing colors). Freshly cut willows, such as the American willow, often have a nice, richly varying coloring from butt to top. There are always barked willow baskets on the market from foreign countries such as Portugal, showing very beautiful, colorful bark colors. Unfortunately, these natural colors do not stand up well to light, so that their original splendor soon fades. After a few years willows get darker; when kept clean they maintain a nice gold ocher tone. If they come into a sooty or dusty environment, they may turn a very dark brown, which has nothing to do with their color, but rather with the substances in them, such as tannic acid, and probably is caused by the all-coloring iron. Even the beautiful warm brown shade of ocher in the

Malacca and Bondut reeds finally fades to a hay color, a grayish olive tone. Splintwoods also yellow, but this takes place imperceptibly and therefore the possessor is scarcely aware of it. It is attributable mainly to the high resin content of the pine. Among the natural colors of the willow is not only the color of aging, but also the nice fox-red of the willows boiled in the bowl. Willow boiling can be done in any season.

Barked willows of various kinds with their own colors, likewise peeled white ones, even sulphur-bleached, buff and perhaps also brown-colored or overcolored willows, offer a rich palette for colorful formation of full willow work. Just by dividing two natural colors in different ways in position and quantity, many kinds of effects and impressions can be achieved. The checkerboard weave, even randing with two colors, makes rich patterns. For that it is only necessary to obtain types of willows that do not lose their bark too easily. The otherwise so outstanding American willow is easily peelable, even in its natural sprouting bark around Pentecost, as in its winter or cooking bark. Unfortunately it has this in and of itself good quality even as a stored, barked weaving willow: the bark gets frayed easily and does not hold onto the wood. Other willow types with colorful bark, whose color is very long-lasting and durable, or scarcely changes at all, because their bark is hard to remove, are harder to obtain. Barked willows are apparently not fit for good society, likewise slewing of short willow tops. But from both, if the work is well done, a nice basket of friendly appearance for home use can easily be conjured up.

The smoking of willows with pyrogallic acid, a developmental coloring with iron content, similar to the photographic silver bromide developer, brings out many kinds of brown tones. If one colors white or red willows with good light-resistant tar dye to a strong golden yellow or orange and then oversmokes them, one gets a warm or orange and then oversmokes them, one gets a warm copper tone that lasts. In the so-called smoking, the willows are dampened, then dipped into the properly thinned, originally colorless pyrogallic solution, dried, and finally put into the sulphuring or smoking chamber. In it is a porcelain bowl of ammonia, whose fumes then slowly develop the pyrogallic acid to a light or dark brown. This process is similar to that in which buff willows are sunned, moistened, then sunned again after their winter bark, and also similar to the bleaching of Cuban palm leaves in sulphur fumes, so that the copper tone, the "fox color", the darker, faintly greenish brown develops. Hazel skeins are likewise colored brown by cooking and adding minerals with the bark, and then mixed sparingly with white hazel skeins, often not in the right place. In the catalog of the burned Seeler-Sachs collection of carrying baskets a dark brown is listed for many baskets. It can scarcely have been a complete coloring of the basket or a bark color, but rather that already mentioned aging color that is associated with soot and dirt.

Natural coloring with dyestuffs that are in the bark and wood, as in willow and hazel, or that are cooked out of herbs, herbs, barks, roots, flowers and fruits, has the great universal advantage of being appropriate for weaving wood. Today, of course, it is possible to obtain excellent, lasting tar dyes or metallic salts that can be mixed to make more delicate shades. But the natural colors that are found everywhere have a delicacy that is inherent in the natural materials too. The danger unfortunately exists of using the splendidly glowing tar dyes, that are easy to color with and in part even fadeless and thus tempting, all too generously out of childlike joy.

Difficulties of Cell-Material Coloring: the weaving plants consist mainly of cellular material, as does linen. But linen can be dyed naturally only with difficulty, and willow also repels the natural plant colors. Let it be expressly stressed here that color—especially in lively types of weave—is not really a weaving means, and is therefore to be ranked last among them. The basket weaver is compelled by the limited range of colors to depend on weave, material, form etc., and to develop these as highly as possible. It is even a very worthwhile artistic exercise to compare natural and restrainedly colored woven wares with such overpowering bright colors and evaluate the two.

The Types of Coloring Procedure

Coloring can take place in various ways, apart from the already mentioned developmental coloring or sulphur bleaching. The major possibilities in the coloring process are:
1. Dyeing the ready-to-weave material in bundles or loose, or dyeing the completely woven basket without decorations, with noncovering colors.
2. Applying covering colors or colored lacquer by painting, spraying or dipping.
3. Partial painting is also done; thus just particular parts of a basket were brought out in the old Schwalm area of Hessen.

Badly and too loosely woven wares, such as are sometimes imported by the carload today, can be made somewhat closer and firmer by spraying with nitrolacquer.

The noble, splendid sheen of the wax layer of the barked willows, or the subdued silkiness of hand-drawn pine splints, is a coloring of its own.

Leathering—Decorating—Trimming—Painting

The unifying of weaving materials with other natural substances is no modern-day invention, but is as old as most in the weaving art. Wood bottoms, leather carriers or belts, metal decorations or clasps have long been used. But they are almost always a sign that the maker has not fully mastered the means of weaving, either technically or artistically, since he had to turn to other materials to finish his work. After World War II the technically unnecessary union of several materials, especially in household goods, was completely rejected for a time. But the need for decoration that many people have had in any era—one need only think of the richness of the old imperial city of Nuremberg, which spread out to the smaller cities and villages in its territory—has always led to inherently good and beautiful weaving work being "decorated" with foreign materials without needing it. The leathering of basket borders or feet was necessary, though, to protect these parts if they were only woven. This technique spread from Franconia into Bavaria, where particularly rich leathering was done, as is still to be seen today. There were Nuremberg egg baskets whose upper rim (wreath) was only woven and others whose rim was lightly covered with leather and sewn with leather thongs. And the rich hop growers demanded richly and broadly decorated egg baskets for the carriages of their marrying daughters. The leathering protected the rim and also the upper body. The stitched overlay of leather was also sewn with colored leather or with fine leather strands and ornamented with peacock-feather stripes (forming initials and numerals of

262–266

the year). There was also a shopping basket, with cover and handle, in two forms, one of which resembles a quartered apple and was carried on the arm against the hip.

Today, unfortunately, there are no more such bridal processions and carriages. In the Franconian Alb the Nuremberg egg basket with all its splendor and beauty became a cherished possession of the future housewife and farmer's wife.

The decorations of these baskets were so rich that for a long time the Bavarian homeland museums did not want to accept simple unleathered baskets. That can be explained: the luxurious, colorful leather decoration took one's attenrtion away from the weaving work; then too, most people can only think in straight lines. Here almost all the surfaces were line drawings in color. The surface as such was not noticed, much less the basket's shape, its form. The artistic form of the basket weave itself remained unnoticed, one looked only at the decoration, which any capable housewife or embroiderer could have made. So
258

today, except in the Bad Windsheim Homeland Museum 259 and at the Trade School, no Nuremberg egg baskets 261 without leather decorations are to be found. And in all the Bavarian homeland museums, above all in Old Bavaria, there is not a single native carrying basket. By way of making excuses, one might yet remark that the old leather colors were not as greasily gleaming as the present-day ones and therefore were closer to the original quality of the basket.

The embroidering of baskets spread particularly in the 194 Biedermeier Era. The presumably oldest form of the so-called "Puppertla", which was placed in the Trade School's collection around 1904, must have been made no later than 1780. It is decorated below with somewhat faded silk embroidery. Later simple small baskets were made with sieve weaving (tapestry weave). The Basket Museum possesses a spoon basket colorfully embroidered with wool yarn in the old Biedermeier style, and in contrast to it an identical but undecorated one that was probably left over from the last production run.

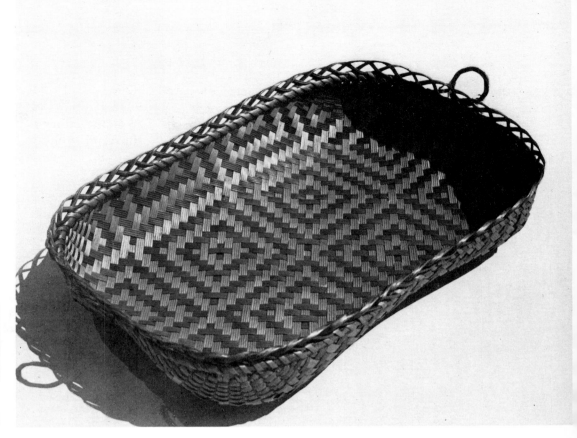

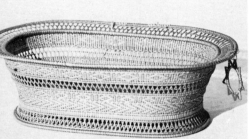

51. *Fruit or bread basket, common Upper Franconian work of fine willow skeins, from the time between 1840 and 1920. The body is randed (before 1, behind 1, or over 1, under 1) and in part also lapped and twilled.*

52. *Pastry bowl with light border, double twill stroke decoration of hand-planed grooved skeins.*

53. *Tray of willow stalk skeins, border hoop of stick skeins, two-walled. Upper surface strongly three-dimensional, lower surface flat, crossbound border fillets.*

54. *Two bread bowls, spiral work, black and red natural colors. Central Africa.*

55. *Sardinian spiral work, raffia bast over round flag, raffia colored by tar dyes, not very lightfast color. From the Isle of Ischia. The creative liveliness of these ornamental designs has been maintained to the present in Sardinia.*

56. *Spiral work, Central Africa, partly woven over with colored straw.*

56

The Extent Of Basket Weaving

Extent in Germany and Neighboring Countries

The Upper Main land, the chief German basket weaving area, includes the Counties of Lichtenfels, Coburg and Kronach. It has stood out for a good two hundred years for its weaving versatility, caused not least by the flexibility of the Upper Franconian basket industry. The fine willow skein work has spread out from there.

The rest of Franconia is also a land rich in baskets. In the ancient mountain chains, as in the limestone areas of Upper Franconia, there has been much basket making activity, which developed toward Middle and Lower Franconia. In the isolated, purely agrarian districts of this strip of hilly land with its steep cliffs, high plateaus and granite summits, new areas of weaving have developed again and again, and have also lasted comparatively long. In the limestone area between Weissenburg in Bavaria and the Hesselberg the unique "Huckelkerm" or back baskets originated, which are still made today, though in smaller size. An unusual type of decoration is found on them here and there, still pure folk art, in which special filed striking hammers are used to hammer into the rear post of ash geometrical designs, stars, crosses, diamonds etc., which basically resemble those stamped into leather-bound books with gilders' stamps. The once finely formed 232 pointed berry baskets of the Fichtelgebirge and the 235 Coburg willow baskets of the Bamberg area also deserve 249 mention here.

The Bavarian Woods, whose ancient stone mountains and hills stretch on to Stifter's Bohemian Woods, are 86–95 likewise still to be included among the areas where splint baskets are created in our own day. It is one of the strange, almost mysterious qualities of good basket making that it, like the spirits of the earth, has drawn back into isolated mountains and woodlands, moorlands and untraveled meadowed valleys. The art of preparing the wood, brought from the North to new homelands as far as South Tirol, is revealed in the splint baskets, whose preparation requires a loving relationship and age-old familiarity with the wood.

The Rest of Bavaria and Swabia: in Old Bavaria itself, except for the Upper Palatine and Lower Bavarian Woods, basket weaving scarcely developed, and when it did, it did not last long. The Ingolstadt Bog, with its late-founded Electoral Bavarian towns of Karlshuld and Karlskron, was a basket-making area as long as industry did not need to hire the small landowners there. The rich hop-growing land of the Hallertau had made excellent use of splint baskets from the Bog. It is strange that, as was already noted, in the numerous Bavarian homeland museums all the way into the depths of the Alps, full as they are of a wide variety of other objects, the carrying baskets of the land are not to be found.

Hessen was rich in woven goods before 1920 and even later; the prosperous farmers of the Schwalm particularly 131 preferred them. The ethnologist Dr. Rudolf Helm, as Director of the Ethnographic Division of the Hessian State Museum in Kassel, had Hessian basket making thoroughly researched and documented by August Gandert after 1933. The excellent collection of woven work in the Germanic National Museum in Nuremberg was also extended and superbly displayed by Dr. Helm. It was lost in the war.

Other German Basket Areas: until about 1950 there were still a number of other areas with weaving activity, such as the Westphalian Weser district of Dahlhausen. Here, in addition to gradually dominating cheap woven goods, very striking willow work was also done. Thuringia also was once a rich basket-making land. There were formerly many makers of willow baby carriages there; later they were even of rattan. Little Schmalkalden, now called Pappenheim, was, among others, a place of outstanding fine hazel and willow work, and the Goethe House in Weimar still preserves, among others, an upright basket for the handkerchiefs that the Minister used for his hay fever and other ills. The Thuringian weaving artists exported their beautiful fine-splint carrying baskets as far as the Hessian and Bavarian Rhoen.

The Erzgebirge too was waiting with excellent splint baskets when the limestone and primitive rock regions of East Central Germany were rich in woven wares. The 234 stumpy pyramidal carrying baskets of Southern Thuringia, staked with full willows and woven of willow skeins with rich decorations, stand out among them. Widespread in all of Germany were the very old bee basket and baking bowl work, both made of wrapped straw rolls for retaining heat. Now as then, bee baskets are the most useful type for beekeeping, and woven baking bowls for the raising of bread dough. But modern man thinks he can no longer use them, because both require much work in making, as in using. The once often-used fish baskets and fish weirs too were replaced by cord and perlon. The fisherman is no longer linked with them by making them himself.

East Germany has not fared differently, for there too technology has driven out the old hand preparation.

Austria, after Switzerland the most mountainous land in Europe, with its granite hills and mountains along the Danube, still has many capable masters of the weaving art. In all the Austrian states basket weavers are at work, and simple but artistic woven wares are produced. In Styria the peasant basket weavers make their carrying baskets, big bowllike pans made of straw rolls and fine-planed barked willow skeins, with two sewn-on handles, for carrying fruit.

South Tirol can still produce many basket weavers and characteristic pieces, even though their splint sieves are no longer woven. High up in Stilfs, "Kirm" and back baskets are still made, as well as fine larch splint and root baskets. But there as everywhere, the old weaving art is declining.

In Switzerland and the other Alemannic lands, such as Alsace and Baden, basket weaving was also once at home. Bowl making was widespread in Switzerland, likewise straw basket making. Outstanding carrying baskets and carrying bands still admired today, finely worked by rope makers, were found in the Fifties. A special art of straw weaving had developed in the Canton of Aargau. The golden gloss of rye straw, the toughness of the fruit-bearing blades, led to the breadwinning production of straw borders and other equally artistic fine-quality utensils in incalculable quantities at home during the long mountain winters. The zeal of appreciative collectors has kept this beautiful and splendid work alive for posterity.

In Alsace too, many a basket is still to be found, as that old borderland has been able to maintain its urban and rural culture into our own day.

The Netherlands and Flemish Belgium were once very significant and rich weaving areas. Many art galleries possess works that show a rich store of willow baskets that can be duplicated very exactly and easily. That great market painting by Pieter Aertsen (1553) can be noted, in just one part of which some fifty baskets are to be seen, a shining example of the old appreciation of baskets in The Netherlands. The land must have been a veritable paradise of weaving. The Netherlands Rural Institutes have gathered extensive collections of woven work and

57. Boy with willow birdcage, old hand drawing from the Netherlands. This type of work, with other bindings, has been maintained to the present in France.

can show very thorough botanical research results, especially on the Malayan rattan.

France too, with its population of Celtic, Germanic-Frankish and Alemannic peoples, is not at all poor in woven goods. The areas on the upper Marne, the region between Besancon and Langres, and the Jura are basket-making localities; the French State Trade School for Willow Growing and Basket Making stands in Fayl-Billot, on the through state highway to Paris. It is the home of beautiful, light, graceful staked full willow work, whose precise bindings must be the delight of every basket admirer. French basket furniture construction, advanced by capable and sensitive designers, achieved significant heights without its forms becoming overly strict. Bowl making along the Belgian-French border, as well as in other isolated areas, was formerly quite widespread. One can still see it in many pictures, for example in French princes' prayer books, where bowls, carrying baskets and fences are frequently shown. The former Director of the Trade School in Fayl-Billot, Jean Fondeux, had begun to gather French woven goods and weaving antiquities for a future museum, for in France too basket weaving had been reduced considerably by technology.

Italy, with Lombardy, Tuscany and the coastal islands, but most of all the weaver's paradise of Sardinia, is a land of old culture, rich in woven work. The Basket Museum and the Trade School possess almost three hundred pieces from Sardinia alone. Among them are very original creations, such as the processional palms, in which the long palm leaves have their shorter fronds plaited with each other in a way that arouses admiration, or the charming and lovable spinning distaffs made of the strong canna tube.

328
332 In Sardinia every girl who wanted to get married had to bring a good dozen woven articles for all sorts of household uses into the marriage with her. To some extent this custom still applies today.

The weaving that still exists in the "Langobardic Lombardy", in Milan and its surrounding area, is well worth a visit. Likewise the Abruzzi can well be visited for the purpose of studying the weaving there.

Spain and Portugal are still important exporters of willows and willow goods today, and also of nice splint baskets. Woven antiques of high quality ought to be found there too.

From England, around the turn of the century, a wave of renewed interest in all areas of handicraft and folk art spread quickly to the Continent and provided new inspiration for weaving there too. On the island itself many types of work and sorts of wares have been preserved that are unknown or have died out on the Continent. The "English lace", an outstanding type of short willow work, has already been mentioned. Corn-ear weavings, which go back to the old Celtic-Germanic custom of sacrificing to the gods, demons and earth spirits in artistic form, were obtained for the German Basket Museum by the far-seeing Mr. von Seidlein of Munich.

Denmark, Sweden, Norway, all of Scandinavia has an ancient weaving culture. The oldest evidence is probably the woven ornamentation of the Oseberg Ship, but beyond that many relics have remained to be preserved in the homeland museums of these countries. The North Swedish woven fences, so similar to those in Carinthia and South Tirol, have already been mentioned.

363–366 Finland is famous for its birch-bark work in which the art of preparing the material correctly has reached a true mastery. Weaving with very broad materials, skeins, splints and palm-leaf straws, is a special process that requires its own types of weaving and binding. And the types of wares that are made of birch bark in Finland are

not exactly everyday things, for example, bath blocks for rubbing off skin, sandals, half-shoes and boots, rucksacks 430 (a kind of book-bag), bottles for salt, bowls, flower vases etc.

Russia seems to be poor in terms of basket weaving, in contrast to the vast extent of its flatlands and the richness of its natural resources, for only seldom are charming and ethnically valuable Russian woven goods to be seen. But this impression may well be attributable to the fact that publications on the subject of Russian weaving are not known in the West. Perhaps pieces of genuine Russian weaving art will appear and be directed to the Basket Museum.

Poland has a population that knows and loves music and creative art. As long as industry does not inhibit handicrafts there, outstanding woven work will still be produced there in a number of areas. The willow plantations laid out and cultivated in the formerly German districts are being carefully preserved by the Poles. The Polish Trade School in Kwidzyn, which is also a technical college with at least four-year training programs, founded after 1945 and built by outstanding designers, has at this time about four hundred students, particularly from agrarian districts. In the city of Rudnik alone some ten thousand people engaged in basket weaving were counted. Through the perceptive and strong leadership of the Director, Josef Szczucinski, this school may well have become the largest basket weaving institute in the world. Professors from the Warsaw College of Art and other creative artists work closely with the school and develop innovative weaving methods that have led to some completely new types of woven wares.

Rumania also still has a creative population that has used an extensive realm of weaving plants—one need only think of the rushes and reeds of the Danube lowlands—to produce many woven goods that have been exported to West Germany in large quantities.

Yugoslavia is, like Poland and Rumania, one of the chief exporters of woven work to West Germany. When parts of what is now Yugoslavia belonged to the old Austrian Empire, much was done to help the very poor population. One of the thirty Austrian weaving trade schools and teaching workshops was established in Apatin, where the cultivation of willows was introduced and carried on. From this city, and again after 1945, the spread of basket weaving was promoted vigorously, so that after just a few years all of Central and Western Europe was so flooded with woven goods from Yugoslavia that the weavers, on account of much higher salaries, were no longer competitive, and many learned basket makers had to move into open positions in other professions, particularly industry.

Hungary, Czechoslovakia, Bulgaria and Albania, the other Eastern Block states, have no present contact with West Germany in basket weaving, although the Slovaks and the mountain folk allied to them, as well as the artistic and handicraft-oriented Hungarians, might have much to offer.

Basket Weaving in Asia

The woven work, from the simplest to the most artistic, that is done in Asia, especially in the Far East, exceeds everything that has ever been known of such handicraft achievements. For thousands of years highly talented artists and artisans have woven there.

In the Near East, Asia Minor and North Africa, especially in the Arab lands such as Egypt, Tunisia etc., very beautiful and colorful woven goods are produced, particularly of wrapped straw rolls, but also of esparto. North Africa in particular, representing its high culture of olden times, has a very fine weaving and coloring technique, yet these splendid, colorful objects rarely reach us. Since straw can be dyed easily and strongly, because its silicic acid skin layer gives a gloss to the colors, so that they scarcely appear to be dyed, "painted" colors, but rather colored lights of unbroken illuminating power, many combinations of colors have a remarkably strong effect that is quite bearable in the bright sunshine of Africa. It is surprising that, on the other hand, the leading rug-weaving countries, such as Turkey and Iran, produce so little woven work. It cannot be caused by a lack of creative power, for ceramics, metalwork, architecture and, as mentioned, textile weaving are at the highest level of handicraft art. Yet there are mosques in Iran that are woven, and indeed in rolls, as boats are elsewhere. Windows and doors also include light or heavier weaves that turn up in endless variations in ornamental construction too.

The Far East, as already mentioned, shines with a simply endless wealth of weaving arts. China is still a country that exports excellent and varied woven goods, kept alive by an ancient culture. Just what it produces in woven work made of cornstalks or the like fills every connoisseur with astonishment again and again. Admirable energy is blended there with great sensitivity and rich, inexhaustible inventiveness.

The building of basket furniture with the Indonesian palm reed and rattan has so developed in China, especially in Hong Kong, that imports of both parts and particularly richly decorated complete basket furniture of all kinds now overflow the Federal Republic and, indeed, all of Europe. Along with that, the most varied products of native basket weaving are produced of all imaginable materials, such as willow, bamboo etc.

Japan, an ancient land of high culture, has been lost to us as a place of basket weaving. What the German Basket Museum, the Lichtenfels Trade School, and other states and museums still possess of Japanese weaving art and its vigorous formative power makes one sad that Japan, in following the trends of the times, has let its worthy old handicraft arts die out.

India, Korea, Tibet, Vietnam, Nepal etc. are likewise countries of great weaving wealth. Technically valuable, yet simple, well-designed utensils developed over hundreds and thousands of years are made there. These are, of course, partly or wholly decorative, but every job of binding and building is done splendidly. There is still no division there between sober utility and living beauty.

The Indonesian islands are a magic world of basketry. Armin Artmann, master basket maker of Untersiemau, near Coburg, was active there for several years as a developmental assistant. He once reported that in a walk across the fields he saw many farmers plowing, each of whom wore a different and more beautiful woven hat than the last. He felt a burning desire, even a duty, to buy all these hats. There was then no mass production there, just as, for example, the Styrian farmers, each in his own way, not only weave their own storage baskets, but invent their own willow planes.

Basket Weaving in Africa

As in North Africa, the other areas of that great continent where weaving is appreciated are very much worth noting. Among almost all African tribes we find a 375–37 high culture, with nothing forced, nothing artificial, nothing simulated in the woven work produced by them, whether the simplest things for daily use or cult or festival objects. Noble forms, excellent weaving and binding in fine total construction, as well as splendid coloring without exaggeration prevail. What the nameless women achieve in weaving and decorating the baskets deserves the greatest respect.

North and South America

These continents can be regarded in weaving terms almost exclusively on the basis of the work of their native populations. The finely formed, rich and deeply felt 58 woven goods that the Indians have created can be placed among the best works of all previously mentioned weaving artists. The North American museums are full of the most beautiful woven work, and many collectors have obtained unique works of art from the Indians and their wives, and preserved them for posterity. It is noteworthy in this respect that the Basket Museum in Michelau possesses the finest plaited bottles from Sardinia, the ornamentation of which is remarkably similar to that of the Indians. The woven baskets and bowls of the Indians are outstandingly formed and follow, whether consciously or not, the laws of spiral work in their formation. One sees not only mirror-image symbols but also, even more appropriate to spiral work, space rotations on the usually circular basket shapes. The North American ethnologist Mason notes a wealth of outstanding basket forms that, despite the monotony inherent in fine wrapped spiral roll work, bring to view fluid pictures growing out of the innate look of the weaving. The story goes that a businessman asked an Indian weaver how much one of his beautiful baskets cost. The latter named a low price in dollars. To the further question of what the cost per piece would be if an order for ten thousand pieces of the same design were given, the Indian shook his head thoughtfully and then named a much higher price per piece in large series production. Naturally the businessman was very surprised at this, for him, incomprehensible rise in price, and wanted to know if it shouldn't be the other way around. The answer was that the work would then become so boring that one would have to be paid extra for it. Here civilization is opposed to culture.

The weaving work of the Latin American Indians is in no way inferior to that of the North Americans. Mexico, for example, produces splendid woven work. The fantastic creations of figures, for example, that are nevertheless appropriate to the straw or rushes, are evidence of weaving art preserved from ancient times and practiced now as then.

Australia and Polynesia

To judge from works in museums, at least, the great continent of Australia has only few woven creations to show. On the other hand, Polynesia, that widespread island world, is particularly fond of weaving. Many woven works in ethnological museums prove this.

Branches of Basket Weaving

Because of the great extent of this subject, only the branches of basket weaving customary in Central Europe can be dealt with here. Their division in basket making handicraft work cannot be made according to individual viewpoints and reasons, but rather according to the most obvious designations for each branch.

Full Willow Work

This branch of work deals mainly with complete, unsplit willows. Stronger willows (an exact limit to their thickness cannot be established) are used in large-scale 105 work, that is, for large objects not always intended for table and household use. Small-scale work can also be seen as part of the production of "small basket wares". Among the main types of full willow work we must first define the so-called green struck work, which uses unpeeled, thus barked willows. These must soften for two weeks before they can be worked. This work, with naturally colorful shades of willow bark and with neat construction, can look very cheery and be thoroughly suitable for the home. The white struck work, that is, the use of white-peeled, often even sulphur-bleached willows, was often done of old by the Hollanders. The profession of the so-called white basket maker is already thousands of years old, but was first mentioned in the Upper Main basket making area only around the middle of the Eighteenth Century. The Romans also knew it for a long time. The buff work, the weaving of whole, peeled buff willows, is just like white struck work in terms of work processes, weaves and bindings. Yet, for example, laundry baskets, in which wet laundry is often put, are not made of buff willows, because they could discolor under some conditions. The so-called willow tops, short growths of very tough types from poor soils, were used only in buff form.

All willows, like all woods, must be stored at least a year so as not to shrink. Weaving freshly cut willows, still in sap, can only be called bungled work.

Fine Willow Skein Work

The willow skein produced by the Upper Franconian basket maker's hand plane, on account of a certain 222 softness, allows many types of skein work that are not possible with either rattan or bamboo. The largest and coarsest masses, as well as the finest, are suitable and workable. Profile planing is native to it; it was invented in Michelau. By this is meant the round and grooved planes; the former give the weave a pearly appearance; the latter allow a lively use of the simplest randing weaves. The aforementioned flat skein weave is only a very simple randing weave, but the relation of the skeins to the vertical stakes allows the extraordinary appearance to come out. Whereas in the ordinary randed skein weaves the flat side of the skein, the planed side, lies vertical and is pressed against the vertical stakes, in a flat-skein weave the flat 319-2 side of the skein lies horizontal, touches the stakes only with the sharp edge of its cross section, which forms part of a circle, and cuts into them a little. This explains why willow skein work, as opposed to full willow work, can achieve incalculably more weave patterns with its types and variations of large and small differences and is thus classified as classical fine weaving work.

Mixtures of Materials: One might presume that, similarly to birch bark work, only one kind of weaving plant would be used in only one type of preparation, only one width and thickness and only one cross-section. But this is not at all the case, since in many kinds of staked weaving the ribs, the stakes or upsetters of the weave, must be stronger than the randing willows to be woven on them. If one wants to attain a certain pearly effect of the weave, then the stakes must be planed in the usual way, but the randing skeins must be drawn through the round 374-37 plane. For certain techniques and types of work, though, any kind of limitation is unnecessary for artistic reasons, because not every material can meet every requirement or fulfill every purpose. In Germany it is no longer possible to bind spiral work with straw, that is, to make the inlay and its wrapping likewise of straw. The Jews of Yemen do straw weaving, as do the Turks, in which inlay and wrapping (binding) are both of straw. For that, though, especially tough and, above all, pull- and tear-resistant types of straw are needed, such as grow only in hot countries. In Germany, on the other hand, one has had to make straw roll work for hundreds, perhaps even thousands of years, with an inlay of straw and a wrapping of willow skein or hand splint, in order to create good and

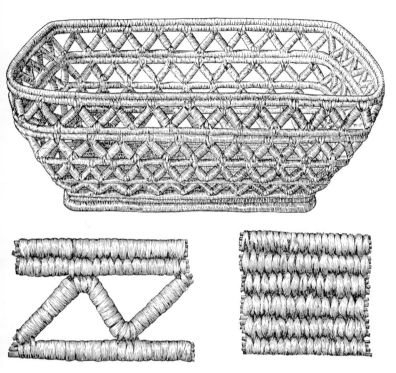

58. Light Indian wrapped roll work in zigzag form (see #270, 275, 276, 302). Also common on other continents, in Europe, for example, in Austria! Done in the Fichtelgebirge with fine pine splints.

durable work. Meanwhile the need for progress and variation, especially in trade and commerce, on which the basket industry depends like any other branch of the economy, has required the mixing of the most varied weaving materials, including the already mentioned artificial ones. But even without these more commercial requirements, certain weaving materials, such as the soft, thin Cuban palm leaf, require a firm weft if baskets and bowls that can bear a load are to be made, so that in this case two materials, from Cuba and Indonesia, must be mixed and wound together. Such mixtures of materials are numerous, indeed almost inexhaustible.

Hand splint weaving is a very inclusive area of work. Just obtaining the splints is almost a science in itself, since it concerns the technical and physical characteristics of the most varied types of wood.

The types of wares and other possible practices of the splint basket maker are, like other branches, in a steady decline, since as a result of increasing technology the farmers need fewer and fewer baskets. Agricultural work forces have been decreased drastically by machines. Yet the basket makers have neglected to change and, instead of doing rural weaving work, create products for their own and thereby simultaneously for city dwelling use.

Rush, Cattail and Reed Work

Wood rushes can be used for fine weaving work when they are harvested at the right time and dried properly. They were, for example, used at the Trade School as weft in place of unavailable long straw tubes for spiral work with fine pine hand splints, especially for pleasant small bowls and baskets. The sea and pond rushes can be used much more diversely. To be sure, water plants are not as hard and durable as the willow, especially not so tough and firm against friction, but they can offer good service over long periods in the making of man's useful basket wares that do not receive rough handling. The working methods and types of wares that are suitable for most kinds of rushes are much more numerous than is generally assumed. They extend from children's toys, which are sometimes made by hand for immediate use, through many types of useful objects to rugs and mats, to say nothing of uses in construction and cane chair weaving. The last is the creation of chair seats whose sitting surfaces, like those of straw rolls with wrapping, never feel cold, as is the case with wood itself. The many air chambers contained in the rushes do not let them feel cold because they, like willow floor mats, absorb the heat of the human body instead of dissipating it. Egg baskets woven of soft rushes are really splendidly suited to protecting their fragile contents and preventing sudden shocks.

The cattail leaf is scarcely of less versatile use. Bent wooden chair frames imported from Spain, that are spanned with cattail cords instead of rushes, are significantly firmer through the use of cattail straws turned and drilled in the ropers' manner. Maize husks, the tough hull leaves of the fruit head, are much worked, especially in southern lands where much maize is grown. They are easily twisted together into strings and thin cords and woven into many objects, and are also used in spiral work.

The pond reed, also called "Schilf" in German, is not used in the Federal Republic except for soundproofing mats in the building trade. For baskets that do not need to be too fine, it can be used well, even by laymen and amateurs who do not have to turn out great quantities, as long as they have the required handcrafting skill. One must pay attention to the forms of the pond reed, likewise the purpose, the types of wares. Their use in ways appropriate to handcrafting, or in a split and planed condition, is not customary. In Southern Europe the thin reed types are used to make baskets for sending flowers.

Straw Work

374–377   Among all the weaving uses of straw, spiral roll work must be the oldest and most widespread. As a working material, straw needs to be tough and firm. Thus it must be softened or dampened before weaving and finally, lightly netted, put in a moist sack, so that it is not too wet and shrinks slightly. The straw rolls are generally made in round cross-section by being drawn through rings of
102   hollow bone, wooden tubes, sometimes of elder, turned wood (as napkin rings can be) or aluminum pipes with rounded angles near the binding and wrapping place, and are bye-staked again and again so that the rounding and the full-circle cross-section remain even. The evening out
374–377   of the roll end on the upper border of the basket is usually achieved by letting the roll run out, that is, get thinner and thinner, and sewing it in closely with the closed border wrapping. One can also let the roll end suddenly, which is not carelessness but a recognized characteristic of spiral circles, as opposed to concentric ones. Natural peoples are much more natural and straightforward; technical qualities are not hidden, as is shown more openly in basket furniture today, where the nails used to be covered "out of shame" with reed skein wrappings, which then came undone very easily and showed unsightly spirals. At the Trade School these things were recognized and taken care of early. Straw figures, like rush figures, were often made. In the German Basket Museum are Mexican straw works that portray houseboats, churches or Christmas mangers. The ancient Swedish Christmas goats, symbols of a heathen Germanic time, are well known. The Swabian "Straw Witches" too, to which the Christmas stars and decorations of straw can be traced back, for which at times wood rushes are used instead of straws, show that straw work has remained alive widely, as do the old straw bindings, harvest braids and harvest bouquets such as are made by the Neusiedler See.

Straw hats are not woven of straw, even though this term is frequently used. Along with those made of straws sewn together, thus not made by weaving, there are many hats that are woven from bottom cross to rim, in simple or artistic manner. One may think of Panama hats and the like, very fine, light, firm and durable summer hats woven in beautiful shapes, that are worked by hand, usually over wooden forms.

Straw shoes are most welcome in very cold weather, 432 where they form an ideal addition to leather footwear 434 when used as overshoes.

Rattan Work

Rattan is used in very many ways, from the smallest baskets through strong coal and transport baskets to basket furniture and construction weaving. In this respect one should also note the production of carpet and upholstered furniture beaters, once of significance in the Lichtenfels area, especially in the village of Neuensee. The beater makers had and still have their own wooden forms, a kind of nail boards, on which they formed the various types of beaters quickly and evenly. They are actually flat knots with handles, in many patterns, sizes and grades of quality, made of the thin natural reed known as beater's reed. Details of production techniques were kept strictly secret. The sizes range from very large rug beaters to wee toy beaters used in doll houses and sometimes also as symbolic pins.

Making Basket Furniture

It is made in individual workshops for framework and rush burning, but usually together with other branches of the subject, because material types, preparation, handling., ways of weaving and binding, and above all work processes extend from one to another. Everything is dependent on the tastes and fashions of the times.

The willow armchair, once built of good pithy willow stakes and full willows with the addition of willow skeins, has faded very much. In Poland, to be sure, light and comfortable willow armchairs, mostly staved and thus scarcely woven out, are still produced. The woven wood chairs with hardwood frame and weaving of various materials are now extinct, but could come back on the market through clever and timely formation and new invention. The same applies to woven steel furniture, as opposite as iron and willow are. The sitting and lying comfort of basket furniture had to be worked at carefully at the Lichtenfels Trade School in the Fifties as a result of requests from Sweden and the United States. An independent frame of thin perforated tubing with steel staves served for the development of sitting and lying profiles. The so-called shell seats were, moreover, not bowed seat surfaces, but three-dimensional forms which, to be sure, required a considerable mastery of weaving techniques and bye-staking.

Construction, Fencing and Decorative Weaving

These three branches of the profession are closely related, in handworking technique as in application. The term "Construction Weaving" was chosen by the author because there was previously no name for this work, which was taken up anew at the instigation of the architect Krueger of Schwaebisch Hall. In itself it is as old as mankind; the fencing in of a stand of crop, the closing off of the entrance to a cave, the roofing over of a sleeping burrow, the building of house walls of weaving with straw clay covering are as old as the oldest woven baskets, the making of containers.

Fence weaving has been kept alive until today in mountainous regions. Construction weaves as elements of space can be flat, raised, smooth, soundbreaking, rough and space-dividing, thick or light. Decorative weaving does not serve serious, useful purposes, but perhaps store decoration, the decorating of halls for great festivities, and especially on the stage and in films. There, for example, large grids that are supposed to represent wrought ironwork are made of burned rattan and reed staves. Among primitive peoples woven cult objects were and are very common. The Ethnographic Museum in Basel possesses an initiation robe that was draped around the trainee of a mystery school or of a medicine man when he was to be initiated into the mysteries between the mundane and the spiritual worlds.

59. Young mother with woven cradle. Steel engraving (see also #228).

Baby Carriage and Doll Carriage Construction

This branch of manufacturing is likewise not young. In paintings very old examples are to be found; the Christmas mangers particularly catch the eye. The productions run from simple shafted carts with wheels made by wagon-makers to modern, stylish, sometimes low-slung, sometimes high-wheeled baby carriages. Development from hanging baskets to expensive cradles with wooden or woven rockers extends just as far. As the woven baby carriage replaced the earlier cart, so it was replaced in turn by plastic and metal wagons, yet it may well return one day. Doll carriages and doll houses (smaller versions of the real thing), cradles, bassinets and wagons, were often lovingly invented and formed.

Bowl Making

This ancient occupation with an equally old history has also been unable to maintain itself any longer in the face of modern economic circumstances, despite tenacious, lasting efforts to preserve it. It changes nothing that in the course of a nostalgia wave grain bowls were used eagerly and frequently as wall decorations, far removed from their purpose. In bowl weaving the splints of brown willow were once taken off by hand, while the thick trunks were later used in the furniture factory. Later one turned to other kinds of wood that were easier to come by, as the hand splint, which was certainly much better but much more expensive, was no longer feasible economically.

Extinct Techniques

A whole series of weaving techniques has already died out, though it is not always clear what the cause of their disappearance was: the general increase in technology, a certain lack of interest in the work or a lack of capable new personnel. So the beautiful, noble spaced work was lost, also the tedious bound work and the "Buendeles" work are scarcely to be found any more. The esparto or sea-grass work, once much practiced and in demand in the weaving of the so-called "old German" armchairs, is no longer known, and nobody has taken the trouble to write down these working procedures and thus retain them for posterity.

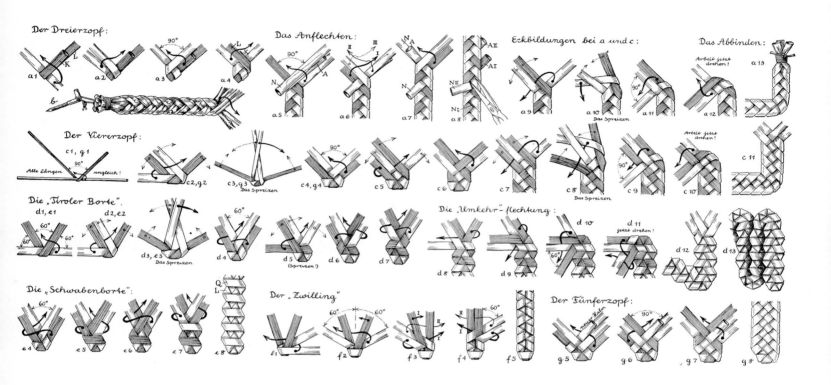

60. *Process of making straw braids and edgings.*

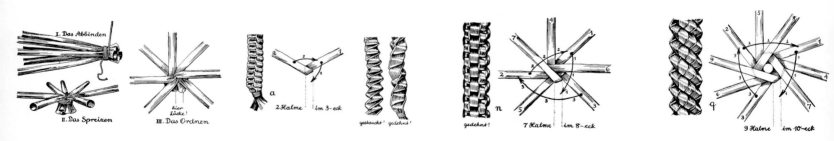

61. *Process of making witches' stairs and cords.*

Types Of Wares And Their Uses

The concept of "types of wares" was probably coined at the Economic Institute of Nuremberg in the Twenties. It means purpose, determination of purpose, type of use or, as is said in other occupations and in the trade, "article". Within basket weaving these types of wares can be divided into main, upper and lower groupings. Even a by no means complete list of types of wares in all the branches of weaving shows some 1300 names, among which the many names and local designations (names of origin) of carrying baskets with in part High German but also dialect forms are not included at all.

The scope of types of use is also very large. Many types of baskets can be used as waste baskets, toy containers or wool baskets. Dish- and bowl-shaped baskets serve to hold bread, fruit, knitting or sewing supplies, small toys etc. Many baskets of rural origin, such as back carrying baskets, are no longer in use in the country; they are used by city dwellers for decorating their houses or furnishing the "peasant room", serve also as wood or paper baskets by the fireplace, sometimes as umbrella stands. In hotels on the Isle of Ischia, for example, ceiling lights have been installed in woven fish weirs in order to create a desired atnosphere. Woven wares of many kinds are displayed, hung on the wall, given a place in the corner of a room, on the ceiling, by a window. One carries baskets in one's hands or takes them lightly by an attached willow ring in the case of small flower baskets or fine pastry bowls. One grasps heavier baskets with the fist, while bowls and swing baskets are held with fingers bent in hook form or with the clenched hand, as the width and size of the handholds provided on them allow. The arm basket is carried on the arm, usually in the crook of the elbow; one can have one on each arm. A heavy, full laundry basket can be carried by its left and right (or front and back) handles by two people, just as the big fodder baskets can be carried better by two people. Woven "belly-loaders" were carried by hastening handlers against their abdomen, hence the name. Many woven pouches, such as hunters' and fishermen's baskets, hang at the side on a carrying strap over one shoulder and lie against the hip. One carries others on the back so as to be free at the sides and have the use of both hands. Fruit and berry picking baskets hang to the front on a belt; thus they are also easy to empty into the large filling baskets. Handled baskets or wide-load bowls and cup baskets with an upholstered straw ring were carried on the head and used to bring food to the fields. This way of carrying is used particularly in the southerly lands of the Orient, and the women are said to acquire their graceful and at the same time proud bearing from it. Carrying baskets, back baskets, simply called "baskets" elsewhere, were likewise carried on the back, some with rope and others with leather belts, still others with flat wooden hoops splinted of short branches. They were carried into the stable by big handles as fodder baskets, or wooden knobs served to hold carrying ropes over the shoulders.

The kinds of wares themselves can be divided crudely into household types, baskets for domestic use, especially the group of basket furniture, which also serves in the garden, baskets and furniture for children and for use as toys, wares for building, for farm, forest and garden work, for trade and commerce, for handicraft and industry, for the restaurant and hotel trade, for stage and film. And there are still all kinds of woven utensil types, that is, woven wares, that can be made use of for many purposes.

The Basketmaking Handicraft In Germany

Weaving was and still is done today on many farms, in limited types of work and only for farmyard use, as had been customarily practiced for centuries. As a handicraft guild the basket makers are among the most recently unionized handworkers. Centuries before them, the carpenters and stonemasons had organized. As in all guilds and unions, the give and take between compulsory guild and free trade was not very advantageous for the weaving artisan. But the order in the handicraft applies to the basket making craft even today, and it is good that way, although a branch of commerce based almost exclusively on handwork naturally has difficulties in withstanding technicalization, salary and marketing problems, the struggle for jobs, and large-scale importing at unbelievably low prices. But now as then, a capable, industrious, talented, highly trained basket maker with manifold ability need not fear a lack of work. He always has plenty to do, he can earn well, as long as he is prudent and flexible.

The Free Farmer, the Half-Farmer and the Independent Basketmaker

In many areas in Germany, as also in Austria, many basket makers practice agriculture in the summer nowadays and work fully at basket making only in the winter. The winter's stock of finished carrying baskets, bowls, arm baskets and grain carriers was carried and sold from house to house in the warm months. But in our day there are fewer and fewer of these half-farmer basket makers. Most of them now are men in their sixties, who produce back baskets and bowls and do not want to give up this beautiful, natural work. But there are still individual, so-called "wild" basket makers who occupy themselves incidentally with weaving and so earn a little money in their travels. The gypsies have long since given up this business that they formerly practiced frequently. The "Mons-Ziggler" who live in Tirol are roughly what is expressed this way in Switzerland: "The basket makers are not real gypsies. They are a tribe of whom it is said: 'People, put the chickens in the barn and take the washing off the line, the Mons-Ziggler are coming'."

The Basket Industry

Basket Weaving on the Upper Main had already developed vigorously around 1800, but particularly after the Wars of Liberation. For a long time the quantities of production and stock had grown so large that they had to be transported by wheelbarrow in summer, by sled in winter, then in horse-drawn wagons. In the course of this development an association between the tradesmen and the large producers was in time inevitable. The "organization of the Basket industry" (basket manufacture) was founded after the important Michelau basket firm of Georg Gagel had moved to Coburg. So Coburg became the seat of the organization.

The kinds of individual basket firms grew out of natural causes. First there were basket merchants, distributors with a cadre of home-based workers. Then came firms that needed large workshops, especially for building basket furniture; concerns with workrooms, storerooms etc. were founded. Other firms expanded by having their own work done on the premises and also employing numerous home-based workers, and also worked together with independent tradesmen who distributed on their own. Many firms had their own workshops, home workers, distributors and managed their own importation, as well as dealing in basket materials; they quickly grew to a significant size.

Wholesale, Retail, Specialty Shops

The wholesale basket trade was carried on by the Upper Franconian basket industry, which soon also profited from the importation of particular woven wares from foreign lands, at first in order to increase the variety of their wares. Distribution went to specific basket goods shops, which in the basket trade are old establishments. These basket weavers, following an old artisans' custom, developed their shops out of old folding booths, and quite early they already offered both their own and foreign woven wares. The surviving market stands are also related; it was above all the city basket makers who used them. Later came transport by freight wagon, once heavily covered stake wagons with two or four strong horses, now high-piled motor trucks with dwelling space, and with ladders to climb. They come particularly from the basket weaving regions on the Rhine and carry products of their own workshops. There are still a few door-to-door peddlers to be found today; they come from Upper or Lower Franconian willow-growing and basket-making localities as the last remnants of the traveling basket merchants. When one arrives in East Bavarian villages, one still hears the natives say when speaking of the origins of their baskets: "There was a man from the woods; he comes every spring."

Training And Science

The Training of the Basket Weaver

It is largely unknown that basket weaving is still a full handicraft today, with a three-year apprenticeship, with apprentices, journeymen and masters, even overmasters.

The State Trade School for Basket Weaving, in Lichtenfels on the Main in Upper Franconia, was already planned around 1860, but only came into being very slowly around 1880 in the form of a traveling drawing school, until finally, using the Vienna Basket Weaving Trade School as a model, a genuine institute with workshops, experimental laboratories, photo studios etc. was founded in 1904, with extensive willow plantations laid out realistically close to it. The Vienna School had come into being long before, in Imperial and Royal Austria. A Master Puppert from Michelau and a Master Karg from nearby Marktzeuln raised it to great heights under the deserving Professor Funke. At the end of the Habsburg Empire there were thirty trade schools and teaching workshops, which naturally served as examples for Lichtenfels and Michelau. The task of the school, which was subordinate to the German and Bavarian State Ministries for Education and Culture, was first of all, under the distinguished Professor Reidt, the building up of a versatile, trained younger generation of journeymen and masters in all the subjects and procedures of the workshop, willow cultivation, knowledge of the craft and the business, drawing and art instruction leading to experimentation, and the so-called sideline subjects of the trade school, which were taught mostly by faculty from the public school or the nearby high school, because the actual faculty had other, purely work-related things to teach. The school was meant above all to maintain and pass on techniques handed down from the olden days, also to develop new ones and provide direction-pointing models for the basket industry and the basket making handicraft. Thorough research work in all the narrower and wider areas of the weaving art were to be carried on at the school, and not in a small way. Along with that went an extensive and many-faceted collection of woven work from all continents and all times, and for comparison, new pieces from all areas. Linked with that was also the production of a trade paper. In the charge of the publisher Hans Lunz in Neustadt bei Coburg, it represented all areas of basket weaving in word and picture for many years. Thereare not many trade schools of basket weaving in Europe. France, Belgium and Holland had some. But since weaving was declining all over Europe, the schools had to change. The presently flourishing Polish trade school in Kwidzyn (formerly Marienwerder) has been mentioned already.

Amateur Basket Makers

The activity of amateurs in weaving, especially with the easily worked rattan, has increased much today and is spreading farther. There were courses of study held at the Trade School which particularly served the further training and advising of work instructors, kindergarten and nursery school teachers and work therapists. In many publishing houses, instruction books for introductary rattan weaving have appeared.

Museums and Collections of Basket Weaving

Graphic and painting collections offer the seeker many possibilities of gaining inspiration or historical knowledge of the weaving art. That applies to collections of the governmental and public kind as well as private ones inside and outside Germany. What is passed on from them in the form of books, periodicals and calendars helps to keep the picture of basket weaving alive, in order to support the weaving creations of the present. It is primarily the ethnographic museums that possess a wealth of woven wares.

The Lower Saxon State Museum in Hannover possesses many native carrying baskets and other woven objects. The Bad Windsheim Homeland Museum, the Leather Museum in Offenbach, and the Shepherds' Museum of Hersbruck could put together a goodly number of excellently preserved, richly leathered Nuremberg egg baskets, and many another museum has preserved treasures of the kind, such as the Bavarian National Museum in Munich. The basket collection of the South Tirolean family of Dr. Ritz is shown there.

Dr. Johannes Lehmann, the former director of the Ethnographic Museum of Frankfurt am Main, was a special friend of basket weaving and knew it thoroughly. He is also to be thanked for the first theory of weaving binding, "Systematics of Weaving".

The burned, but in part replaced and significant collection of older baskets in the Germanic National Museum in Nuremberg has already been mentioned.

The State Trade Institute in Nuremberg was able to gather old Upper Franconian fine woven work, as well as the Youth Style weaving of the Lichtenfels Trade School, and save some of them through the war. The German Basket Museum, as the only specialized museum of its kind, stands above all the named and unnamed collections for its thoroughgoing photo archives alone.

The museum is in communication with numerous other specialized museums that possess woven wares: the Bread Museum in Ulm, the Farmers' Museum in Stainz (Styria) etc. The Fishermen's Guild of Wuerzburg, more than 968 years old, enlarges its collection of fishing baskets and weirs along with the Basket Museum. The Trade School in Vienna had the oldest basket collection. The Lichtenfels Trade School strove since 1904 to equal it, supported by understanding people (Vogler in Marktzeuln, Aumueller in Michelau). They collected everything connected with basket weaving: baskets of all times and peoples, insofar as they were obtainable (114 back baskets alone), materials, tools, implements and machines, books and pictures. The collection was constantly enlarged. It is rich and very diverse. The German Basket Museum in Michelau on the Main, Upper Franconia, did not come into being without remarkable things. Since 1925 the author gave instruction as a drawing teacher at the Lichtenfels Trade School, as a traveling drawing teacher in various basket making towns, and also in the greatest basket making village, Michelau. He wanted, no matter what, to give instruction in drawing with the help of examples and models, not just with chalk, as at the Trade School itself, and so he asked the directors for such things. The request was refused. The young teacher, convinced of the necessity and rightness of his intentions, then turned to the Second Mayor and basket industrialist and commercial scientist, Dr. Klaus Stammberger, with the same request, that the community might provide models, examples of work and other teaching equipment. Here he received the answer: "No, we won't do that! We'll set up a real museum right away, as we have long wanted to. Make the plans and details for it!" That happened in 1928-29, and in that year Michelau began the collection, though it had grown bitterly poor in the time of unemployment after World War I was lost. Through cooperation, through selfless generosity of the old masters and connoisseurs Fritzheiner, Fritzlas Gorg, Paul Backert as well as the Trade School teacher Lorenz Karl and others, the first possessions came together, almost without spending money, mainly through requests for contributions and in the process of forming a Museum Society. In 1934 the new mayor, Jakob Fischer, likewise a basket manufacturer and a former Trade School student, gave the museum a small home of two and a half rooms in the abandoned city hall, which immediately after its opening came under the direction of the Bavarian State Office for Monument Care in Munich, and found a good friend and helper in its curator, Dr. Josef Maria Ritz, later the Director, who knew the old Upper Franconian weaving art thoroughly. In his tenure great sacrifices of time and money were made by everyone involved, and the names of the collectors at that time, who visited the neighboring villages on foot and bought what they could find out of their own pockets or put their own valuable pieces at the disposal of the museum, deserved to be entered in the Basket Museum's book in gold letters. Today the tasks of the Basket Museum have become more extensive, although the Museum is staffed only with honorary directors, who work together as a committee.

Individual collections, such as the Seeler-Sachs carrying basket collection in Leipzig (with 120 pieces) that was destroyed by bombing in the war, and that has survived only in the form of a catalog, the rich Indonesian and Turkish basket collection of the master basket maker Otto Prischmann in Lepizig, which was gladly and understandingly taken up by a small Saxon museum, the African collection of the Chiemsee academy professor Koenig, the Stainz collection in Styria, set up by Frau Dr. Kundegraber, and surely many private collections unknown here, complete the group of friends of baskets.

Development And Research

Research in Basket Making

Basket making, with all its contents, achievements of the past, tasks for the future and effects, is not to be grasped and exhausted so quickly. At the Trade School experimental work has been carried on under the author, and since 1950 has also been much advanced thanks to E. R. P. funding via the Bavarian Economic Ministry. It has applied to all technical-scientific and practical handworking areas of basket weaving, and should be extended to the formative, commercial, historical and other areas. The Basket Museum too, which has taken over the very extensive archives left by the publisher of the trade paper, "Weaving Work", Hans Lunz, is occupied with research work. But the State Trade School must first of all have the ability to go beyond the momentary work required mostly by fashion and economy, devote itself to basic research and, not merely in the sense of actual monument preservation, to maintaining the old techniques of the weaving art. To this belong, among others, dyeing processes, smoking processes, basket makers' hand plane blades along with their benches, pliers, wood for forms, splint basket making, machines for basket making, gardens of willow types (Salicetum), the invention of suitable veneers for industrial splint weaving, types of weaving for construction work, the construction work itself etc.

Whatever is mediocre and false in the material is also false in the form and the craft, is sacrificed to a short-lived fashion. Everything that is good and beautiful is also worth preserving, whether it looks simple or is richly decorated.

62. *Cutting willows by hand with willow shears when not in sap.*

63. *Low head willow in Styria, Austria; a small spruce also grows out of it (seed blew in). The willow is still used for weaving.*

64. *Willow cutting by machine in winter.*

65. *Willow harvest.*

▽ 64   63   ▽ 65

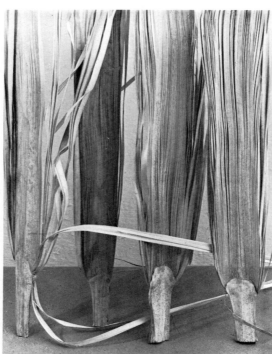

66. Shipping bundles of Cuban palm leaf, in front an open pinnate leaf with capped stalk.

67. Still-closed, naturally folded Cuban palm leaves without stalks.

68. Harvesting the Sardinian hard rush, also exported to Elba and Ischia.

69. Shipping palm reed bundles down Indonesian rivers to gathering places in export harbors.
70. Rattan bundles are loaded onto a seagoing ship.
71-72. Warehouse of a basket material wholesaler (excerpts). #71 left: Manau reed bundles; right: basket willows. #72 back: rattan bundles (palm reed); front: hand-woven mats for packing long reed bundles.

73-74. *Adam Zasche, chief teacher at the Trade School. #73: the old master of the Upper Franconian fine weaving art splitting willows; #74: thin planing of split willows with the Upper Franconian basket maker's hand plane (compare #75).*

75. *Planing willows with an Upper Franconian basket maker's hand plane with side seat.*

76. *Slimming already planed skeins on the step-slimmer. The slimmers are inserted into the slimmer bar of the plane bench.*

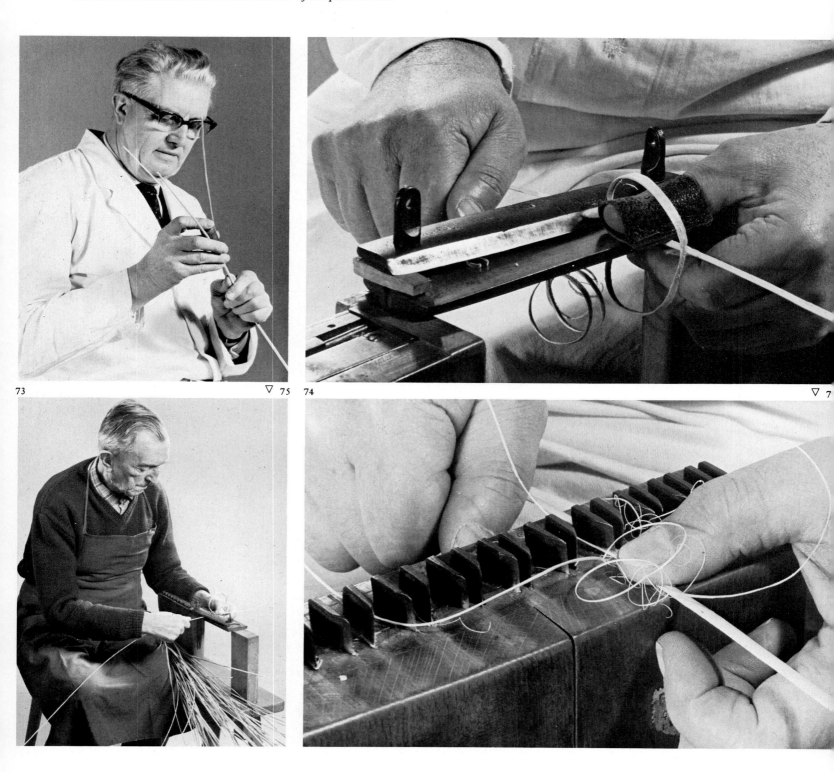

73   ▽ 75   74   ▽ 7

77. Old Thuringian hand plane of elder wood with slim blade. Still in use in 1941. Here the skeins lie in a naturally round bed (grooves). 4o high, 55 long, 70 wide.

78. Seated workbench developed at the Lichtenfels Trade School. The tool compartments are opened.

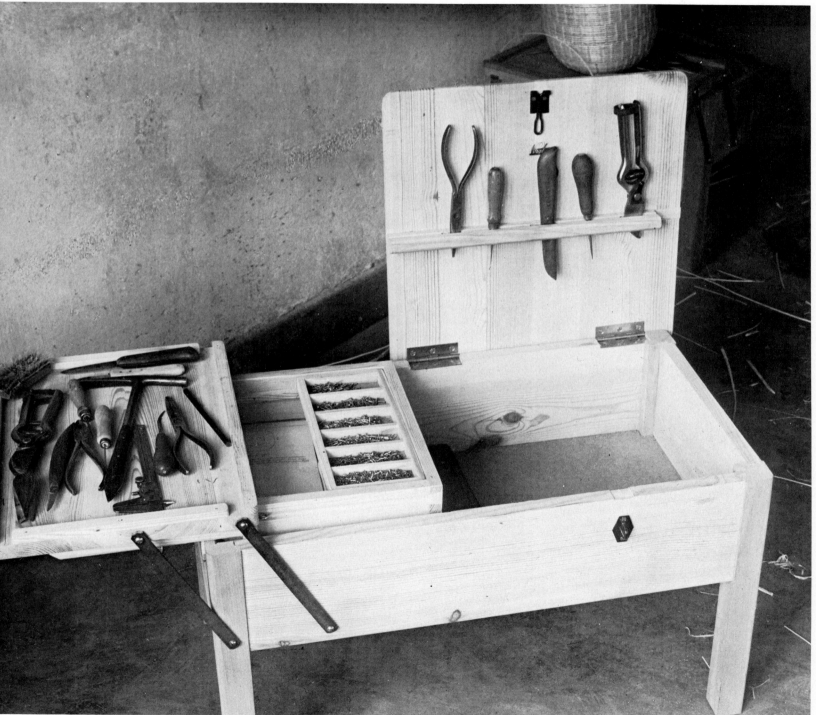

80. *Forest splint basket maker straddling the cutting buck, loosening a strong pine hand splint.*

81. *On the old cutting buck (carving bench) a splint wedge is evened with the draw knife before removing the splint.*

82. *The plaiting stock of the now-deceased fine basket maker in Stilfs, South Tirol. Holding a spiral-work bowl of larch hand splints, 1970.*

83. *Separating buck, with which hazel splits are cracked from the stick, used here to bend preheated Manau reed sticks, circa 1955.*

84. *Hand splint removal by cracking thick hazel splits over a pointed stick held between the knees. Upper Ziller Valley, Tirol, 1970.*

79. *Splint basket maker removing hazel splint*

80   ▽ 82   81   ▽ 83   ▽ 8

86. *Process of making a four-post back carrying basket (Kirm). The flat bottom (high and deep weave) is laid. The basket maker kneels on a board that holds the stakes (ribs) fast while weaving.*

87. *The bottom is pressed into the form usually made in advance, the ribs temporarily bound in place by light sticks. The bottom is held down with the left foot.*

88. *The ribs are bound to the form with helping sticks.*

89. *Naturally brown-colored barked and white-peeled skeins are woven in closed rounds from the bottom up.*

90. *The border hoop of hazel skeins on both sides of the ribs of the finished weave is attached with branch clamps before binding.*

91. *Three-post Middle-Franconian/Upper Palatine back basket (Kirm or Kerm) of wide strong and wide thin hazel or pine splints (also aspen or poplar). Tapped foot frame of split and ordered crossbars, no wire nails.*

86   ▽ 89 87   ▽ 90 88   ▽ 9

92. *In front of a basket shop on the Isle of Elba. Mostly native manufactures. Right foreground: hand splint work of young sweet chestnut trunks.*

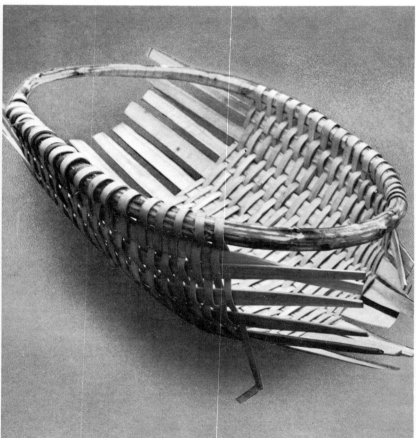

93-95. Work on a bowl or swing basket.

93. The already bent and sharmed basket-round hoop is laid from the middle out with the ribs and the woven-in randing skeins.

94. The ribs (spokes) are fastened with three woven splints. The rounding of the future bowl is shown in the waves of the begun, not yet woven arch. Upper left: the rapping iron.

95. One half of the bowl is woven from the middle out. The spokes are then renewed and pointed outside.

96. A bowl binder, working from the handholds and hoops to the middle.

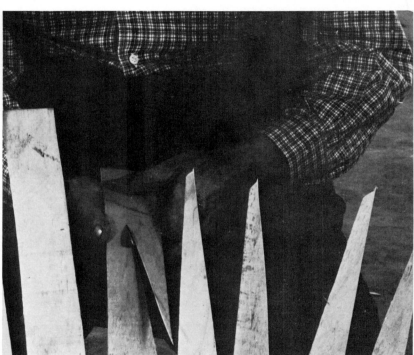

97-100. A Westphalian grain bowl is made.
97. The ribs are bye-staked and woven in.

98. The willows (fine cube or layer willows) are struck (beaten) close together, as long as they are wet and soft.

99. The bowl maker sits in the bowl's bottom on the bench and weaves from inside toward outside.

100. The free ends of the spokes are pointed, so as to be inserted into the weave more easily around the border hoop.

101-103. Making a baked-goods bowl. The beginning of the straw roll is rolled on the work board and fastened with binding strokes of evergreen splints.

102. The straw rolls must be organized and filled out regularly through the ring.

103. The roll has to be laid exactly according to the form. The fingers of the left hand help out.

104. Round rattan work, an elliptically opened-out bottom beginning (6=2+2+2).

105. Elliptical basket, opened-out bottom of white willows, 4=2+2. Weave of layering, cubes, layering and plain border.

101   ▽ 104   102   103   ▽ 1

106. Upper Franconian white willow basket maker works on a laundry basket. Instead of bottom sticks (compare #104,105), a split fillet, smoothed on the cutting board, with holes bored for the stakes. Left foreground: cubed carrying basket, Coburg type, behind it a staved laundry basket decorated with waved fitches.

107. *Weaving a woman's hat of fine white willow skeins. The wooden form is on a stock. The weavers (skeins) must be cut correctly in size and direction so they provide thickness, even if the softened skeins shrink somewhat after drying.*

108. *Sallow wood form, attached to the stock head by a stake. The turned groove is the boundary mark for the beginning of the upper decorative rounds.*

109-112. *Working on a handled basket.*

109. *The bottom star is completed with three fitched skeins. It bears a foot fillet. The bottom has been nailed to the form with small blocks. The weave goes before two, behind 1=3 skeins.*

110. Simple randed body weave, before 1, behind 1, running as in the bottom, upward in spirals to the closing triple weave. The four-ply closing weave is a horizontally even plaited weave, unlike the triple weave.

111. The border wrapped with a skein and the hoop of the handle are provided with an edging for firmness and decoration. Here embroidery and weaving meet.

112. All protruding skein ends are picked ("cleaned up") with the side cutters.

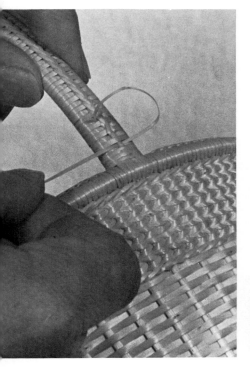

113-118. Bottom types.

113. Crude East Asian bottom of bamboo skeins (split), multiple willow bottom star.

114. Basket-round bottom of pricked-up full willows, opened out of the thin side, woven out with flat skeins. The bottom sticks are stuck through at the edge. Every skein binds the bottom and the foot hoop.

115. Bottom type from the Philippines, rotation, a sort of swirl in which the bottom sticks of cocoa-palm leaf ribs are bent to one side.

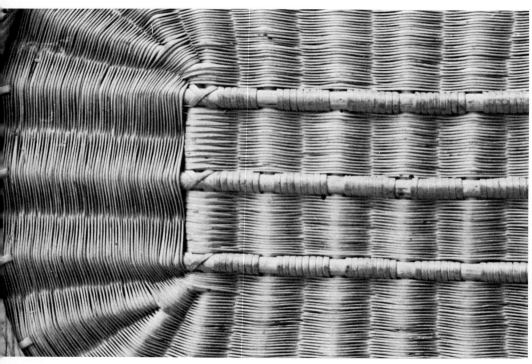

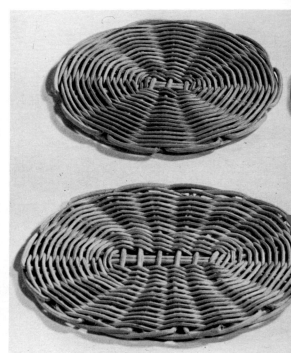

116. Four small basket-round table mats with different axis designs, caused by the numbers of bottom sticks crossing at equal intervals. 180 long, 130 wide.

117. Lightly fitched spiral bottom of Esparto lines.

118. Right-angled spiral bottom, rattan splints with palm-leaf, wrapping and binding strokes. Foot formation by inlaying of round [Ladig].

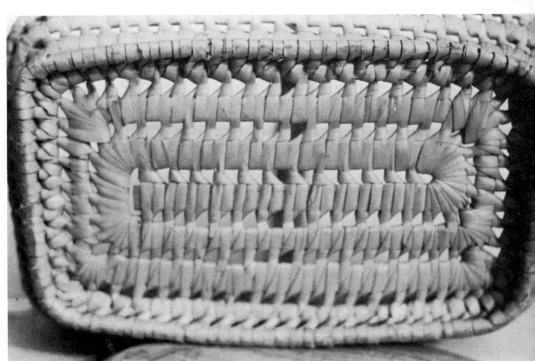

119-130. Examples of stake-woven borders.

119. Simplest rolled border, behind one and forward. There are hundreds of rolled, trac, plain and braided borders..

120. Simplest rolled border, reversed, before one and backward.

121. Simplest rolled border, longer stroke over or before two and backward.

122. Plain border introduced in two ways: before one and backward, behind one, before one, backward. The simplest plain border would be before one and backward, behind one and forward (always two moves into which every plain border is divided). Through the use of different numbers, from one to four, there are endless weaving possibilities. The introduction number is involved too.

123. Numbers reversed from #122, but with three introductions.

124. A plain border with three half-strokes, under one, over two, with two introductions.

125. Every three single stakes are brought together into a line of three ribbons. With only two half-strokes and a single introduction, though, it is simple. Naturally, it could be done very simply as a one-willow plain border.

126. Three-willow line as in #128, but the stroke goes over two.

127. As in #126, first stroke over three. The basic pattern is long: over six stakes.

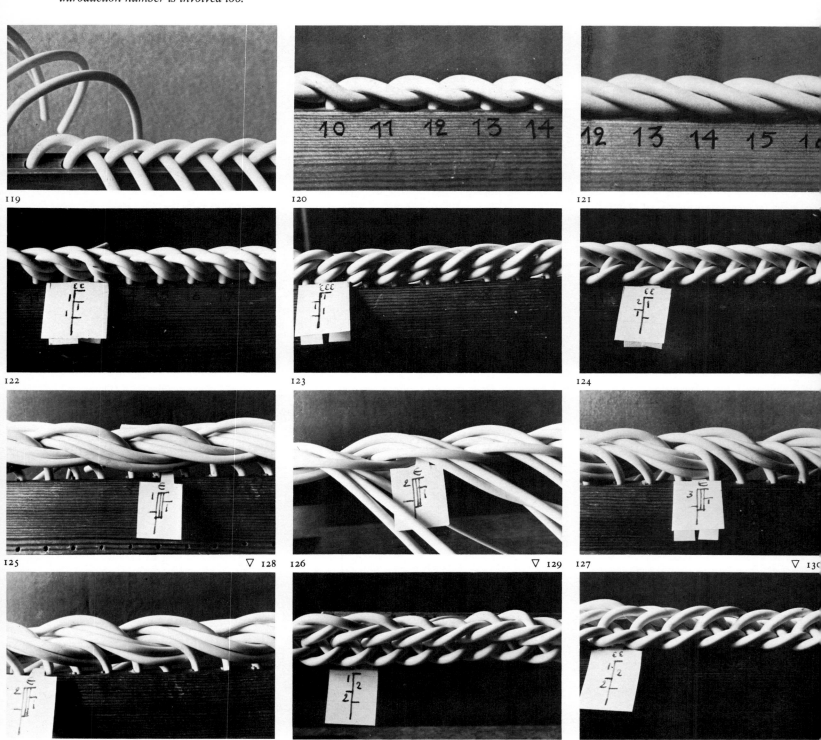

119

120

121

122

123

124

125   ▽ 128   126   ▽ 129   127   ▽ 130

128. *Three-willow plain border with one introduction. Two half-strokes before two, behind one, forward, otherwise as #125-127.*

129. *Plain border with two introductions, before one, behind two and forward, before two and backward. Front view.*

130. *Like #129 but seen from above. There are closed borders that, seen from above, look like others seen from the front. The changing power of the numbers in the weaving has not yet been worked out. Instead of working by unpictorial numbers, the highly trained weaver could imagine the stake border appearance he wanted in terms of visible stroke lengths and means of weaving.*

131. *Mending or laundry basket from the Schwalm area of Hessen, full willows, partly painted, overstaking of the body weave, rich light border and foot, always of two willows. Middle rounds of body and lid are of willow skeins, circa 1930. Height 300, length 520, width 354.*

132-145. *Types of construction weaving.*

132. *Basket weave, suitable for construction weaving when enlarged or coarsened, 1954 and later.*

133. *Wide and narrow rattan bands, bound with fine rattan skeins. The back is shown in #135.*

134. *Light four-ply construction weave with rattan band bound to the stakes crosswise, each bordered by a fitch.*

135. *Back of #133. Here the diagonals take the form of lively diagonal cross strokes.*

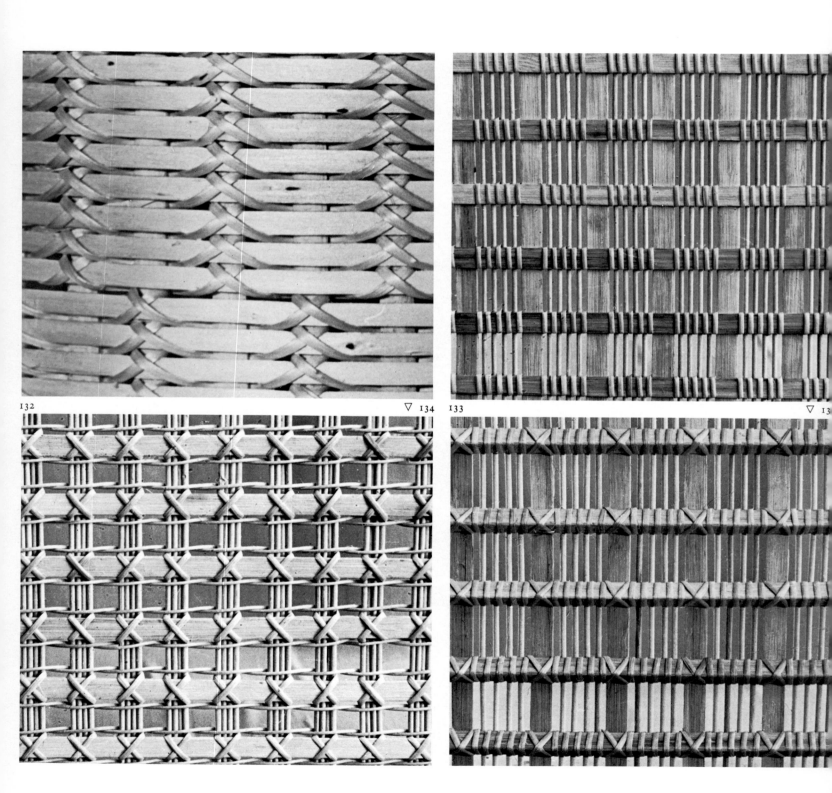

132

133

△ 134

△ 13

92

136. Markedly projecting 'rough' construction weave for dampening sound, made of wide thin plastic skeins fitched in a particular way.

137. Triple weave of knife splints (can also be made of plastic).

138. Light knotted construction weave of transparent plexiglas, hard stakes, softer slings.

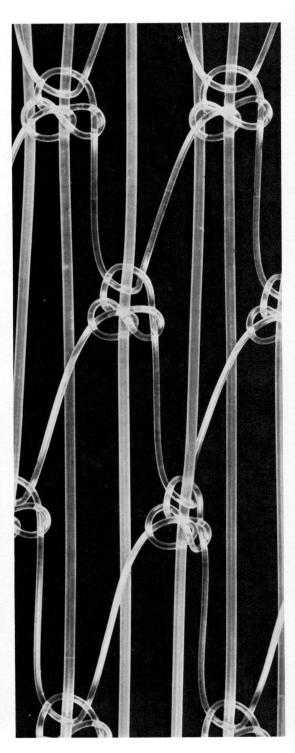

139. *Hung construction and basket weave, similar to fine hosiery knitting, simplest basic weave, but rich in content and variable in many ways.*

140. *Construction and border weave of natural reed skeins, crossed and bound with skeins.*

141. *Rich hung weave of round rattan (compare #139).*

142. *Border and construction weave, similar to #140. The variable width is achieved through weaving means.*

143. *Drawn-out two-colored hexagonal weave, finest execution with six directions.*

144. *Light hexagonal weave with six-pointed stars, partly twined out.*

145. *Like #143, made larger.*

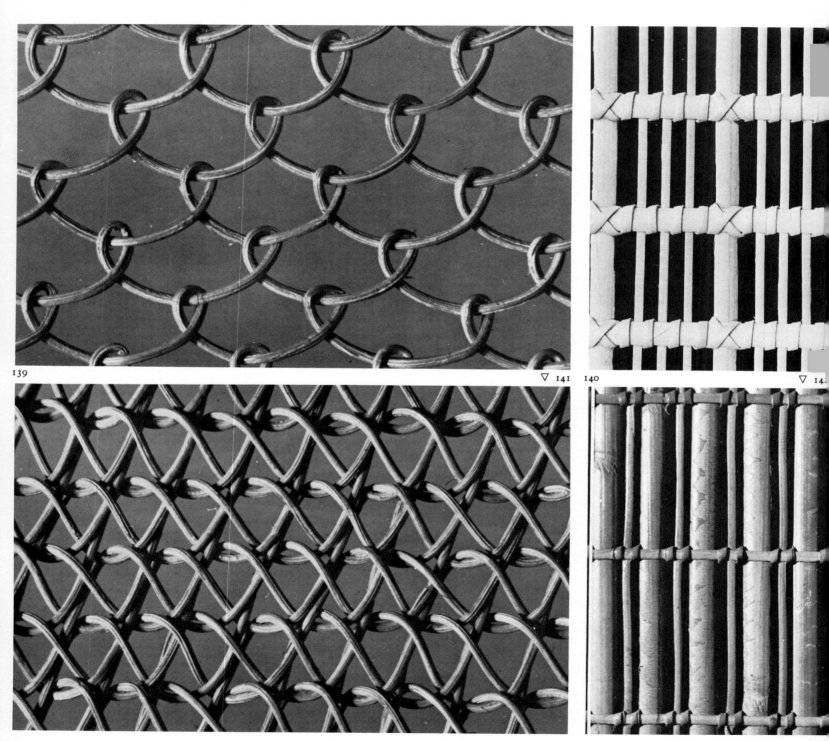

139

▽ 141   140

▽ 14?

94

146. *Ring fence on the Rosskopf above Sterzing, South Tirol. Slabs split on the spot.*

147. *Old barn, now demolished, in Lichtenfels, Upper Franconia, woven panels were covered with straw-dung clay, covering has partly fallen away. (Compare #1).*

148. *Gate fastened with spruce-branch rings.*

149. *Woven panels in the old part of Nuremberg, near the Duerer House. (Compare # 1 and 147).*

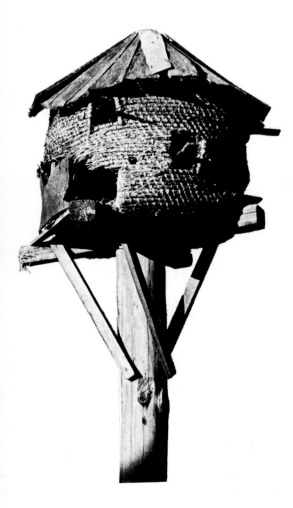

150. Dovecote of wrapped straw roll work, faulty building and fastening.

151. Old straw-roofed barn, uncovered woven panels (compare previous pictures).

152. *Village fence (above Sterzing, South Tirol), split slabs partly woven; in front of it a carrying basket. The fence is hard to get over, thus protects well and is cheap (compare #4, 12, 155).*

153. *Deer fence in the high mountains near Sterzing, fits into the landscape without disturbance.*

154. *Ring fence (compare #156). The spruce branches are warmed over a fire so they bend more easily.*

155. *Forest fence (compare #151), randed and crossed only above, badly made or badly maintained.*

156. Diagonal ring fence, near Sterzing, South Tirol (compare #154).

157. Garden fence, woven by Rumanian war prisoners in North Germany, excellent work.

158-159. *Grain sieve from Gomagoi, below Stilfs, South Tirol, with radial splint rim. weave of fine hand splint, weaving splints sewn between the rims. The name "sieve weave" comes from the old grain sieves. Height 120, diameter 530.*

160. *Wagon body woven by farmers, ribs set in holes, randed weave interspersed with closing fitches. Faaker See, Carinthia.*

161. Manure basket ("Benne", compare Thuringian "Behnert" or "Baehnert"). Fully loaded manure baskets were pulled uphill on sleds, hence the skid skeins on the bottom, boatlike shape, splint, full willow or hazel.

162. Westphalian grain bowl, ancient form, type of work taken over by the Germans (and Celts) from the Romans. Already known in Ur, Chaldea (compare #97-100). Height 260, length 980, width 808.

163. *Small basket of fine birch bark, Finland. Height 65, length 100, width 116.*

164. *Bottle of birch bark.*

165. *Small basket of birch bark, pointed edge through folding the diagonal weave over, Finland. Height 80, length 80, width 80.*

166. *Containers of thickly woven birch bark.*

163

164

165

167. Food baskets that nest in each other, colorfully decorated spiral work from India.

168. Baskets from #167, completely nested. Height 246, length 240. Left, a colorful African bowl.

169. Old apiary with three beehives, drawing.

170. Beehives, wrapped straw roll work (compare #169). Left hive height 380, diameter 400.

171. Simple drawing of a beehive in an advertisement.

172. Apiary with many beehive shapes, straw roll work, partly covered with straw-dung clay or pure cow manure containing binding egg white and straw bits, for warmth. Bees like straw hives best.

242. *Westphalian back basket, white full willows, for carrying poultry, inset wooden boards or woven intermediate bottoms, unique form corresponding to the bent back.*

243. *Back basket with three board bottoms.*

244. *Back basket, fine willow skeins, main stakes pointed above and* below to take carrying belts, old form, already used in Nuernberg around 1500, height 850, length 240, width 240.

245. *Fodder basket without carrying belt, large high carrying bow handle.*

246. *Basket from #245 carried with a cudgel over the shoulder.*

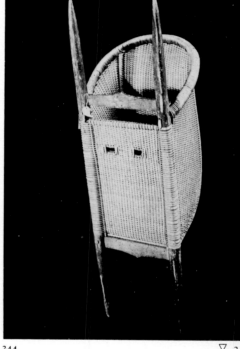

242

243

▽ 245

244

▽ 24

247. *Hessian back basket, wide and narrow splints, ribs set in holes in the bottom board, high back panel indicates style from farther west that presumably came up the Main. Rhoen area, height 880, length 450, width 470.*

248. *Hessian-Lower Franconian weir, lightly upsett, wide hand splints, slightly randed, unique binding of the upper bows to the spokes. Rhoen area, height 800, length 510, width 500.*

249. *Pointed or berry basket, very old form, of spruce and pine splints, no bottom board, bottom made of border and filling, stakes bored through, Fichtelgebirge, height 560, length 390, width 350.*

250. *"Kirm" of straw rolls bound with brown willow skeins, found in Bad Klein-Kirchheim, Carinthia, presumably from Styria, height 460, length 460, width 280.*

251. *Hessian-Thuringian back basket (Kiepe, Koetze), fine hand-splints with two wide fillets with holes for the loops of the carrying bands to pass through, Hessian-Thuringian borderland in the Rhoen, height 615, length 440, width, 390.*

252. *Pointed basket (Kirm; compare #249), with wide, very comfortable carrying belt. Bavarian Woods, height 390, length 360, width 350.*

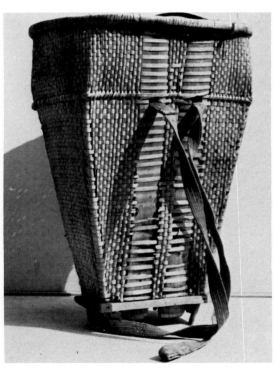

253. Leaf baskets, Ziller Valley, Tirol, for carrying loose leaves down from the hills to village barns for strewing when straw was in short supply. Height of these baskets to 150 cm, width to 180 cm. Hand splints, twisted spruce branches for carrying.

254. Three-legged "Kerm", locally called a "Butte", pine ribs and fine splints of quaking aspen (poplar). Franconian Jura, height 590, length 400, width 390, below 83.

255. Four-legged fodder basket, mortised foot pieces, hoop on the front also provides two posts (corner posts) and a handle (compare #245). Height 900, length 640, width 680.

256. Back basket, board bottom set in, West Franconian style, height 690, length 610, width 460.

257. "Kirm", rear post with a "tail", with small decorations, Upper Austria, in part also common in Vorarlberg, height 726, length 540, width 540.

253   ▽ 255   ▽ 256 254   ▽ 25

258. Nuremberg egg basket, onion shape, from the Franconian Alb circle of influence and rule of the old Imperial City, artistic form, hard to weave, bye-staked with hand splints of various woods (note the lower front corner), without leathering. Height 420, length 442, width 440.

259. Nuremberg egg basket, with protective leathering on the rim, low wide shape. Compare the different widths and intervals of the spokes (ribs) with the woven splints (randing skeins) in #258, 259, 261.

260. Leaf or fodder basket, in foreground a child's carrying basket, South Tirol, Gomagoi near Stilfs.

261. Nuremberg egg basket, wide nut-tree hand splints, back cushion of leather, only the rim leathered, height 366, length 470, width 470.

262. *Arm basket shaped like a quartered apple, hand splints, in part willows, richly decorated with colored leather (compare #264-266), leather covering and sewing with decorations, embroidery with colored leather straps, lid also fully leathered.*

263. *Hand basket, basket-round Biedermeier form of bottom and body, very leathered, decorated with Imperial eagle, circa 1850 (compare #279-280), height 250, length 450, width 324.*

264. *Old Bavarian arm basket, richly decorated with the old Wittelsbach diamond coat of arms and heart-shaped shield, partly leathered, circa 1850.*

265. *Similar arm basket without leathering (compare #262, 264, 266).*

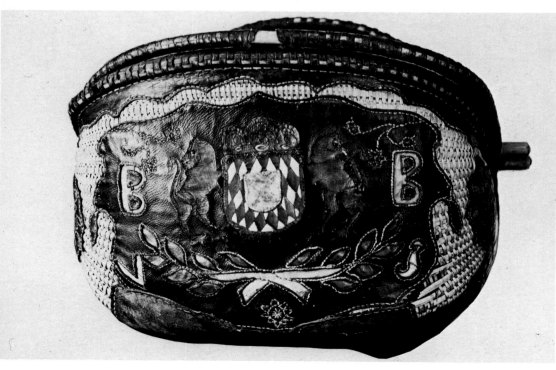

266. *Arm basket, partly leathered.*

267. Two-handled hamper, finest tied work, representing the large Bavarian state arms, colored ties, lacquered reeds nailed on. Height 160, length 244, width 124.

268. Covered baskets with handles, fine willow skeins, differing in having the same weaving (triple weave) on odd-and even-numbered stakes, showing effect of different numbers.

269. Small handbag, special foot shape for good standing.

270. Handled baskets, left spaced work over round rattan or full willow, right fine willow skeins, partly crossed, noteworthy foot formation (compare #275 & 276). Left: height 85, length 226, width 122; right: height 104, length 220, width 112.

271. Small handled basket (arm basket), for use as a lady's handbag with decoration.

272. Handbag (Koberla), black lacquered reed, outwardly horizontal, bound with white whipcord, inside vertical stakes, rich patterns in crossor Holbein stitching.

273. "Koberla", of horizontal black and white lacquered reed, tied with white whipcord, height 120, length 140, width 118.

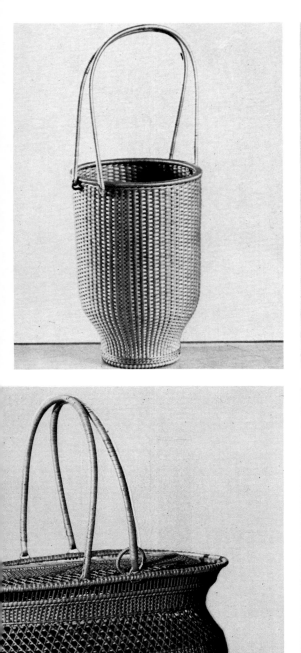

133

274. Fine small arm basket, "Koberla" type, two-tone randing with twilled decorations. Michelau, circa 1860.

276. Small arm basket with lid and two handles, fine willow skeins, Biedermeier style, Tree of Life and bird design in body, circa 1840.

275. Arm basket, very old form, worked of flat skeins over full willow stakes, zigzag foot (compare #270, 276). Height 300, diameter 260.

277. Small arm basket, basket-round bottom and hoop, fine white willow skeins, three-forked handle. Height 180., length 310, width 170.

278. *Two completely leathered arm baskets from Franconia, woven of fine hand splints over rods, form of a quartered apple.*

279. *Arm basket, fully leathered, basic Biedermeier style from Upper Franconia. leathering mainly by local saddlers. Height 280, length 400, width 280.*

280. *Basket (compare #279), partly leathered. Height 260, length 380, width 294.*

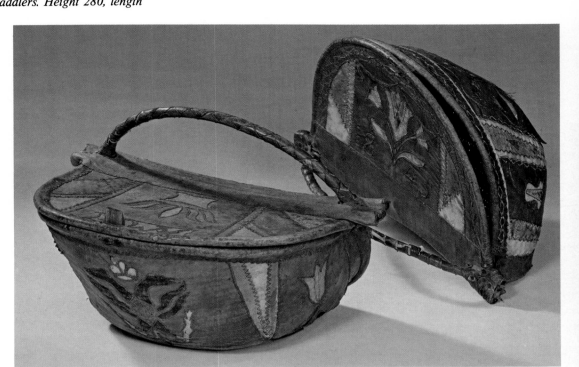

281. *Arm basket, fine white willow skeins, made to an old Biedermeier pattern, circa 1920. Height 235, length 388, width 285.*

282. *Hanseatic maidservant's basket, smallest-detail work with decorative chain, fine white and red buff willow skeins. Height 150, length 190, width 114.*

283. *Hanseatic maidservant's basket, flat skein high cover and base. Height 270, length 324, width 264.*

284. *Hanseatic maidservant's basket with very high flat skein lid and wreath (gallery) on it for holding visiting cards when bottles of wine were given out.*

285. Hanseatic maidservant's basket with bowed rim and diamond pattern.

286. Maidservant from Luebeck, richly decorated shopping basket with double row of chains.

287. Wall or dustcloth basket, crossed (a kind of hexagonal weave).

288. Wall or dustcloth basket, willow skeins, Buendelas work. Height 140, length 160, width 148.

289. Small handled basket, round rattan, special bottom design (compare #401).

290. "Koberla" with two handles, willow skeins, circa 1850.

291. "Koberla", form with folds, circa 1860. Height 180, length 320, width 180.

292. Small hand basket, lengthened octagonal form, fitched staving with handhold and hasp, circa 1835 to about 1900. Height 90, length 164, width 92.

293. Workbasket with two handles and lid, willow skeins, circa 1880.

294. Workbasket with double handle, palm-leaf spiral work, hasp, circa 1900, Mitwitz area, Upper Franconia.

295. "Koberla" with double handle, black esparto, white and black lacquered reed.

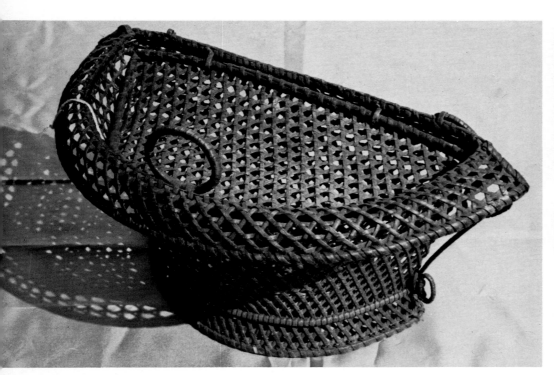

296. *Sewing and embroidery basket, fine white willow skeins, lapped weave, overhanging rim, two handles, circa 1940, Michelau. Height 100, length 290, width 240.*

297. *Shopping basket, white willow skeins, two-lid basket with handle, four-ply rounds between waled rounds (all closed rounds). Height 230, length 380, width 230.*

92

3

294

▽ 295

296

▽ 297

139

298. Two-lid basket, white full willows, willow skein wrapping, cubed body between waled rounds.

299. Swiss basket, willow skeins with high handle for tying flowers on.

300. Basket as in #298, front view.

301. So-called Duerer basket, after a copperplate (Farmers) by Albrecht Duerer, height 200, length 194, width 240.

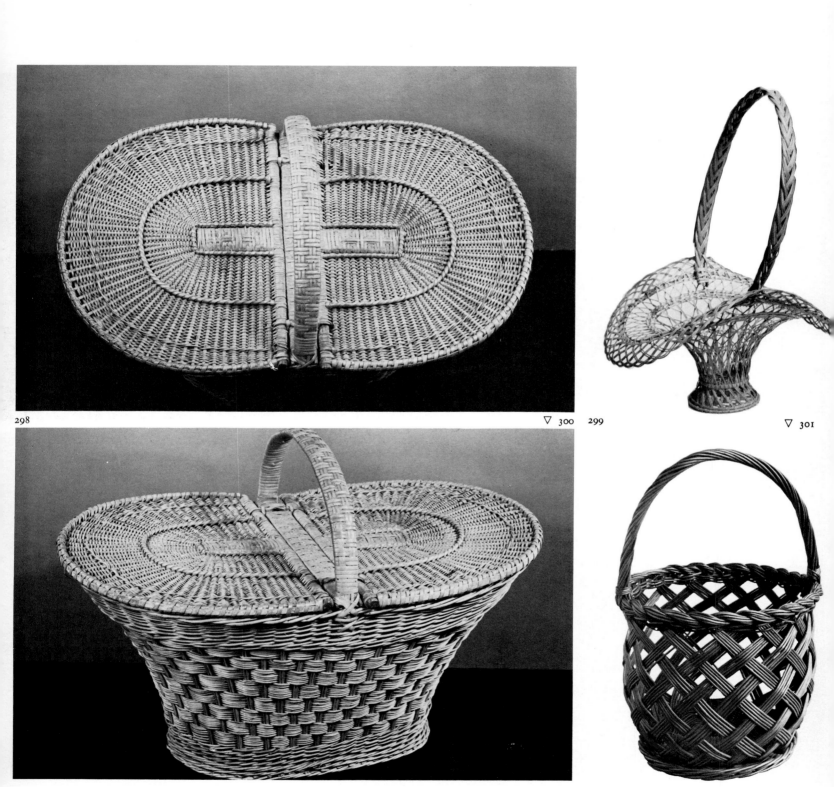

298

▽ 300   299

▽ 301

302. Handled plate, spiral work, fine hand splints over hazel or willow rods, zigzag rounds (compare #63, 275). Fichtelgebirge.

303. Handled basket with lid, hazel skeins, Thuringia. Height 200, length 300, width 230.

304. Swing basket, hazel rods and hoop, spruce root skein weavers, height 190, length 390, width 350.

305. Swing basket, hazel skeins, Thuringia (compare #304), height 90, length 240, width 194.

306. Tobacco basket with hanger (chain), white willow skeins, height 150, diameter 174.

307. Case, round rattan, knots on handle and hasp, rich hung weave, East Asia.

308. Small provision basket, wrapped straw roll work, with lid, pine hand splint wrapping.

309. Ship-shaped swing basket, built up from the circular ring, very old basket design.

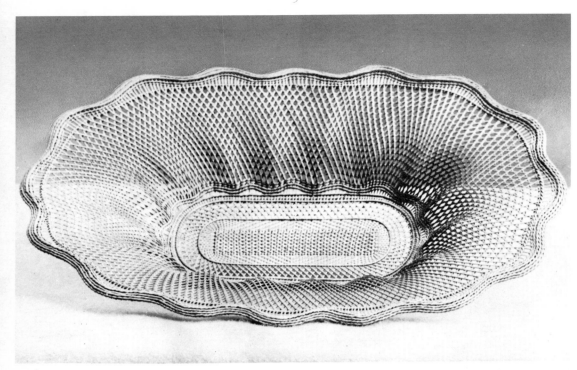

310-311. *Platter with folds, basket-round (plate), fine white willow skeins, height 80, length 450, width 296.*

312. *Big platter, made of fine flat willow skeins over full willows, yellowed with age, made 1933, lost after the war. Stakes first bent in twisted or swirled form, richly plaited rim (foot was of wide willow stake skeins, bound on).*

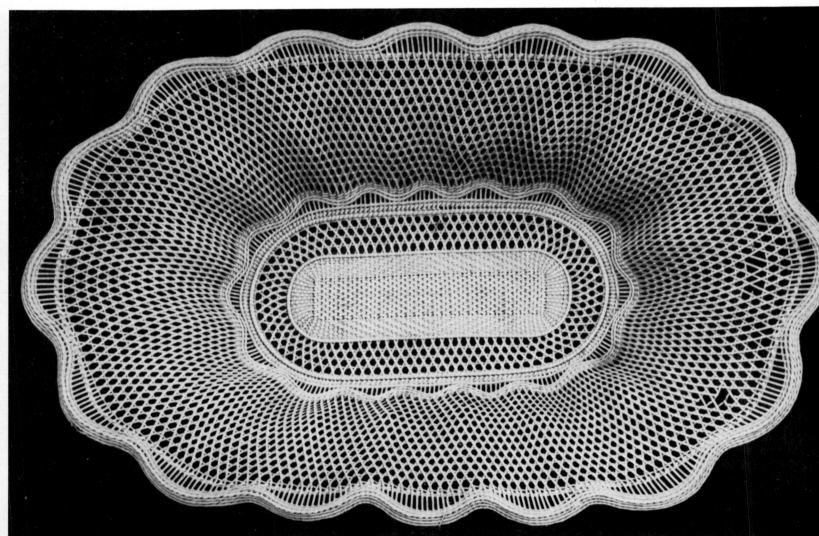

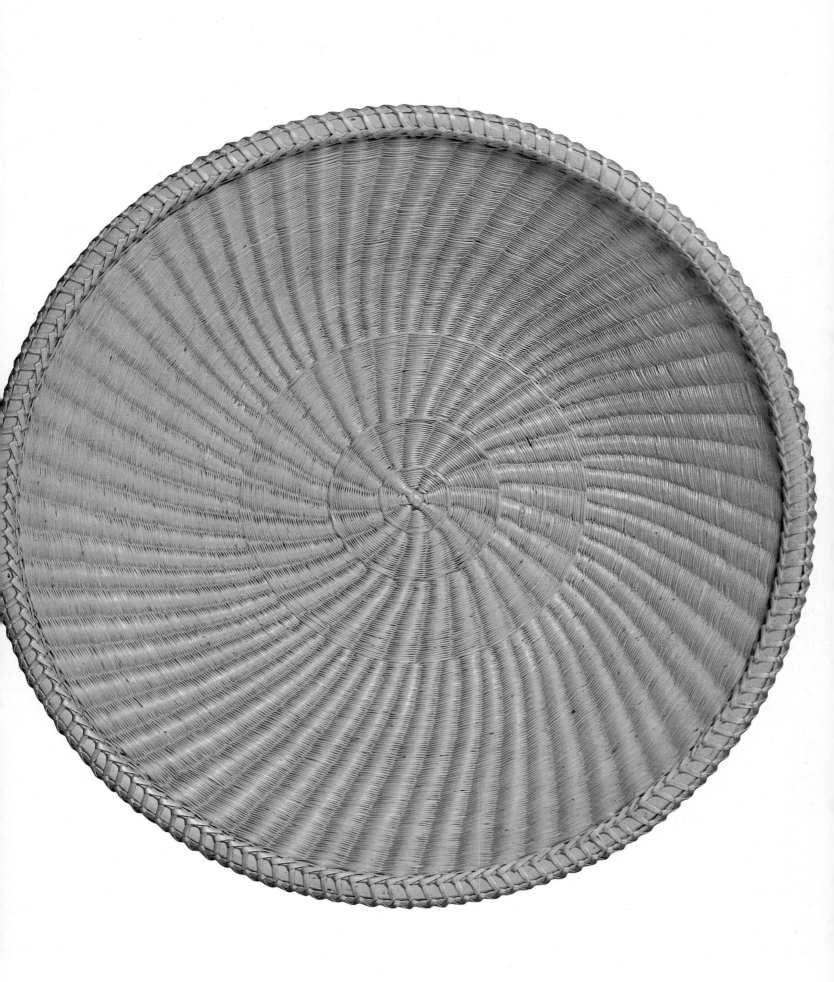

313. Plate with folds, finest willow skeins, rounded rectangular basic form, circa 1860.

314. Elliptical platter with folds, fine willow skeins, bottom of pressed fitches, decorated with twilled strokes.

315, 316. Round plate with folds, fine willow skeins, silvered, staved with double fitches, circa 1860. Height 84, diameter 316.

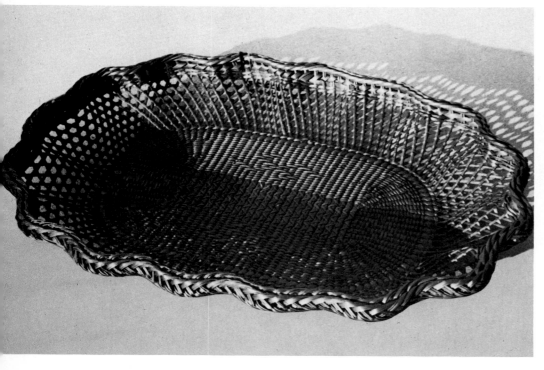

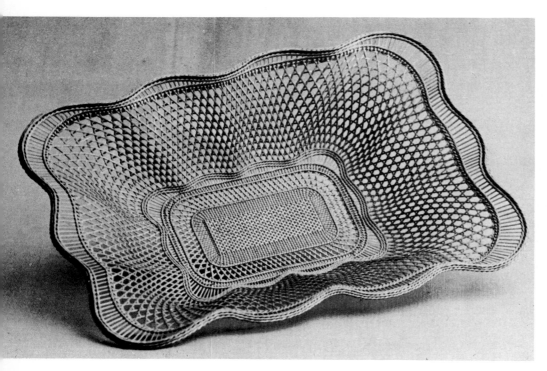

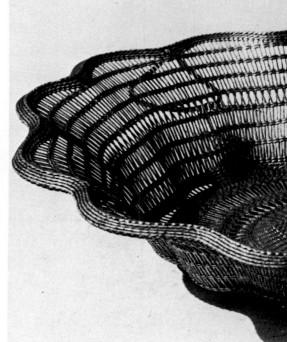

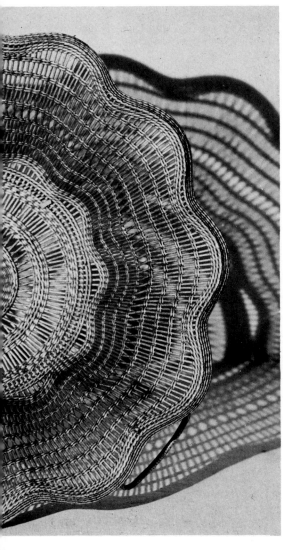

317. *Platter with folds (plate) white willow skeins, yellowed with age, plaited body weave, double willows.*

318. *Round platter, made as in #317, flat skein bottom, circa 1860.*

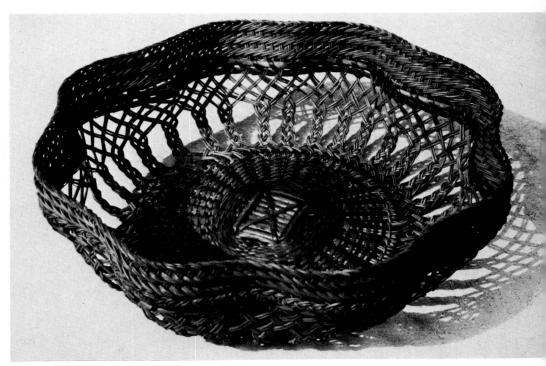

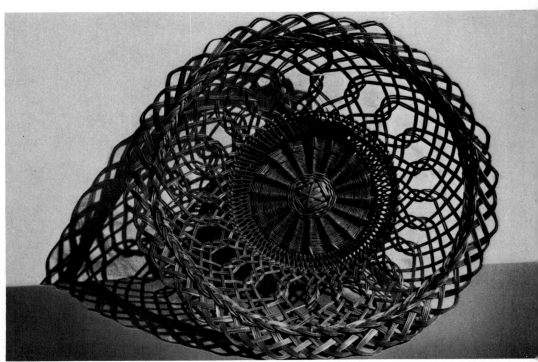

319

319. Round pastry platter, flat skein bottom, crossed body, border with drawn bow, multiple willows. Marktzeuln, length 100.
320. Round bowl with thick border, Marktzeuln type, circa 1840.
321. Round bowl with thick turned-down border.
322. Round bowl, similar to #319, with wide foot, bottom all of flat skeins, height 100, diameter 260.
323. Round bowl, unstaked, with large flat skein bottom, body of hexagonal weave, two handles.

324

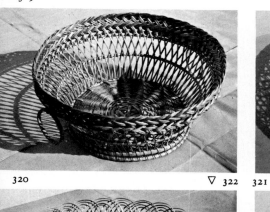

320

▽ 322

321

▽ 323

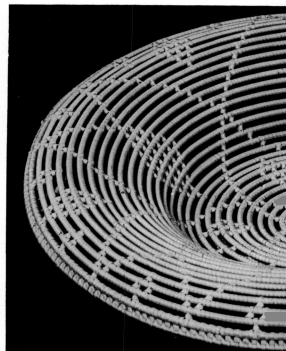

148

324. *Round bread bowl, bound-up bottom square, flat skein weave, top rounds of spaced work in simple pattern.*

325, 326. *Round bowls, arched rails, very spaced, starred rings. 325: height 85, diameter 330; 326: height 42, diameter 208.*

327. *Elliptical spaced bowl, decorated with fish symbols of varying size.*

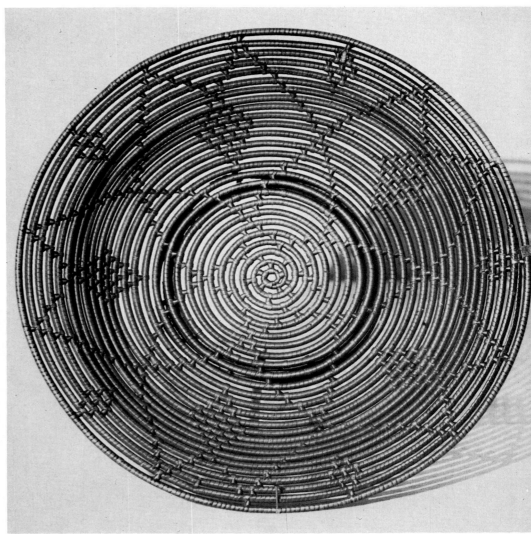

▽ 325 326

▽ 327

149

328. Platters and covered baskets from the old Hebraic enclave of
Sinai, on Sardinia. Finest spiral roll work, Greek plant patterns, fine
natural-color skeins and red felt strips, centers of finest brocade.

150

329, 330. Small African bowl, natural-colored and black hard grass, noble form, running spiral work (partial and complete pictures), height 110, diameter 232.

331. High covered basket with drawn-up decorations, Central Africa.

332. Large bowl, compare with #328, Sinai, Sardinia.

333. Big straw roll platter, pine splint wrapping.

334. Old bowl, spiral roll work, larch splints, South Tirol, height 74, diameter 250.

335. Fruit bowl, straw spiral work, weft of wood rushes instead of forest hair-grass ("Schmellm") or hand-threshed straw, which is hard to obtain today, height 125, diameter 260.

336. Bread bowl, willow skeins, with wide colorful stripes.

337. Fruit bowl, four-willow drawn border and foot, hanging rings, ornamental lower body pattern, old Upper Franconian (Michelau), height 98m length 190, width 120.

338. Japanese bowl, bamboo skeins, colored with katechu, twilled body. Note the solution of the corner feet!

333

▽ 334   335

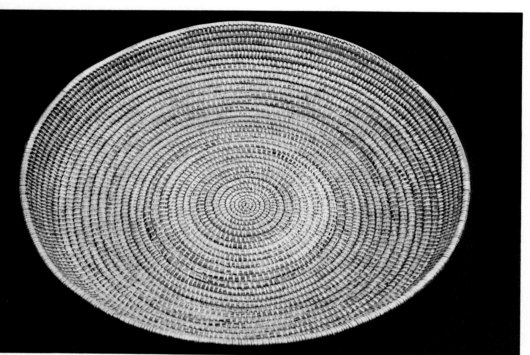

152

336 337

▽ 336   337

▽ 338

339. *Bowl, completely drawn, five willows, six groups.*

340. *Bowl, six willows, six groups, completely drawn, best hard buff willow tops.*

341. *Bowl, five willows, six groups, completely drawn, willow skeins, intervals between groups increases steadily outwardly, held together by bindings at the crossing points, always divided on the basis of 5=3+2, light on a dark background.*

342. *The same bowl, dark on a light background.*

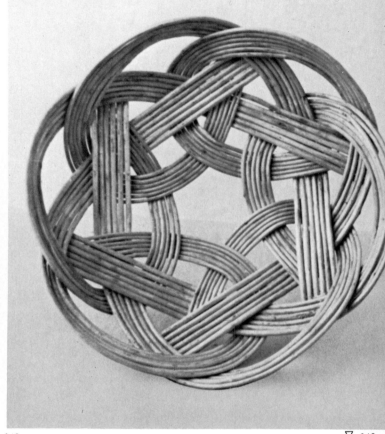

339

∇ 341

340

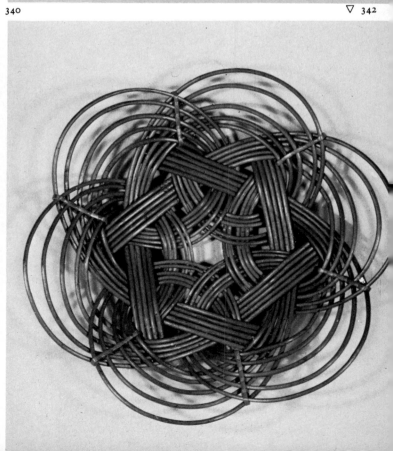

∇ 342

343. *Straw roll spiral bowl, colorful, with symbol in changing colors (scarab?), central field with Arabic characters, Egypt, diameter 840.*

344. *Large bowl with castle symbol in the form of city coat of arms, Sardinian-Hebraic, height 94, diameter 740.*

345. *Straw bowl, wrapped with colored straw, animal symbol in varied colors, inscription in the central field, Egypt, diameter 763.*

346. *Straw roll bowl, woven over in color, Egypt, height 130, diameter 276.*

343

∇ 345   344

∇ 346

347. *Compressed-circular bread tray, red willow tops, bound-up bottom square.*

348. *Elliptical bread basket with new bottom center, buff willow tops.*

349. *Canoe-shaped splint dish, smoked hand splints, Carinthia, Austria.*

350. *Canoe-shaped splint dish with glued pointed ends.*

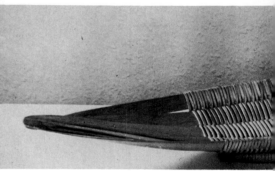

351. Basket-round bowl, old spiral work with laminated fine pine splints, Fichtelgebirge.

352. Bread tray, wedge-shaped splint stakes turned back in at the border.

353. Rounded-rectangular bread basket, splint-work.

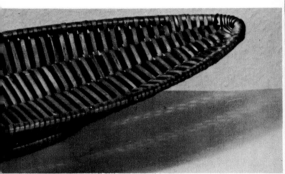

354. *Single-axis mirrorlike bowl, willow skeins.*

355. *Large round banquet bowl (compare #312), willow skeins, flat skeined with swirled stakes (rotational order), diameter 550.*

356. *Master Gerd Backert weaving a round hall ceiling panel (before its mounting in the room), rattan bands over stake rattan.*

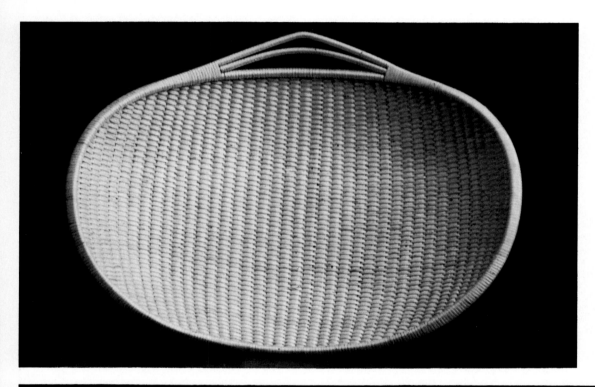

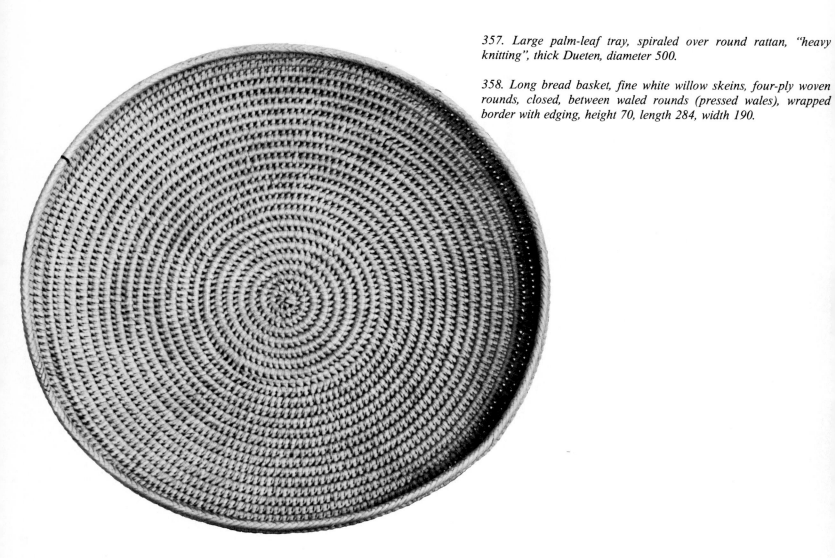

357. *Large palm-leaf tray, spiraled over round rattan, "heavy knitting", thick Dueten, diameter 500.*

358. *Long bread basket, fine white willow skeins, four-ply woven rounds, closed, between waled rounds (pressed wales), wrapped border with edging, height 70, length 284, width 190.*

160

359. Silverware basket, white and dark willow skeins with twill decoration, divided into two parts, Michelau work, circa 1870.

360. Thuringian money basket, hazel splints, divided into six parts, circa 1900.

361. Jewelry box with lid, divided by low partitions into four parts, tray that set inside was lost, wide splint on the top to fasten the flat weave that will not stay without arching.

362. Rounded-rectangular tray, divided by four partitions in rotational order into five parts, willow skeins, height 66, length 212, width 164.

363. Long silverware basket, hand splints, Thuringia, height 44, length 210, width 134.

364. Left: compressed basket-round nut tray, divided into four parts by longer and shorter partitions, one handle, willow skeins. Right: flat circular nut tray, with dual crown handle representing the partition cross and the circular form.

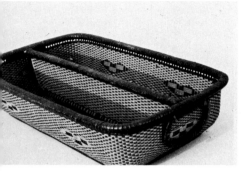

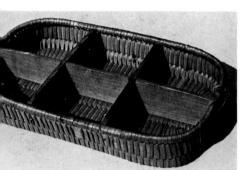

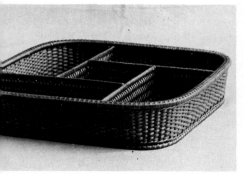

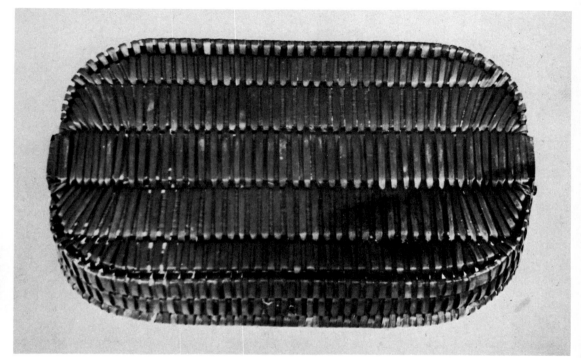

365. *Round flat bread tray, wide thin willow skeins, smoothly wrapped border, laid bottom!*

366. *Rounded rectangular tray, hand splints.*

367. *Canoe-shaped bread basket, willow skeins, height 70, length 470, width 266.*

368. *Bread basket, willow skeins, upright rails, bottom bound up, height 46, length 320, width 195.*

369. *Long bread tray, peeled veneer splints, smoked.*

370. *Burgundy basket with lid.*

371. *Elliptical bread or pastry tray, 3:1:1:1-willow diamond crossings (sieve weave).*

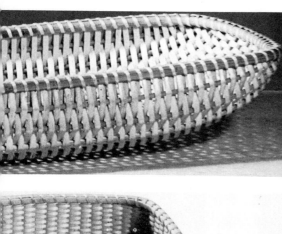

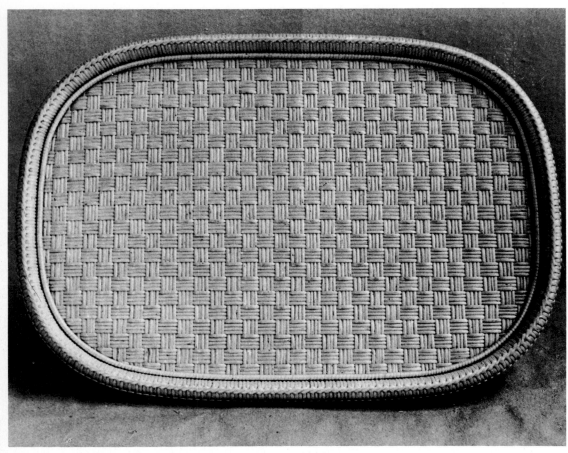

372. *Tray of white willow skeins, flat upper surface.*

373. *Tray, strongly woven underside for carrying (double wall), height 24, length 500, width 360.*

374. Flat tray, straw roll work, circle divided into eighths, pairs of axes in clearly contrasting colors, Egypt.

375. Bread tray, straw roll work, spirals, with colorful pattern inserted on top, Africa.

376. Fruit bowl, natural colors, red and green, wrapped work spiraling to the right with three-color decoration, likewise continued in orderly swirls and rotations, India, height 240, diameter 430.

377. Hat of spiral work, three natural colors, insets and transitions careless but always made in the same position as clearly recognizable jumps, Central Africa, height 206, length 275, width 260.

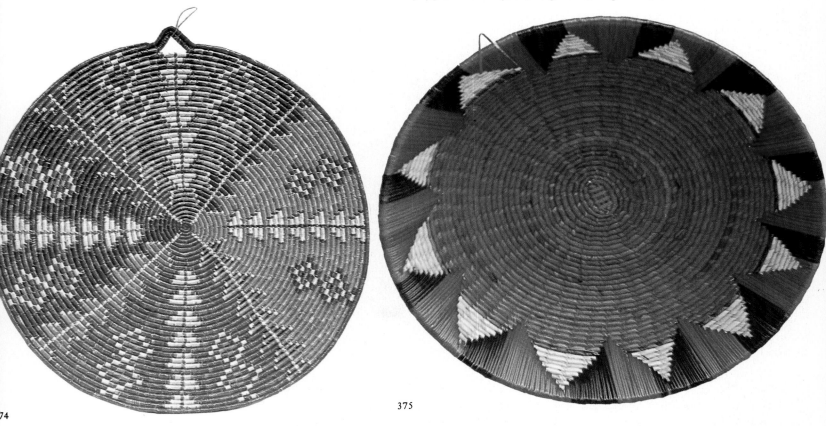

374

375

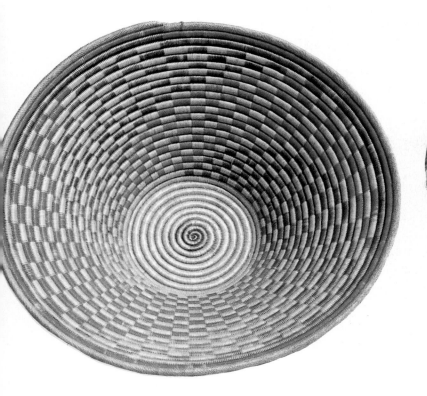

376

377

165

378-382. Examples of twilled patterns with diamond dividing lines.

378. High basket, Indian type of work.

379. Twilled basket, finest weaving, zigzag twill (portion).

380. Cylindrical covered basket, vertically ascending zigzag twill, top with twilled diamond pattern (with filling).

381. Covered basket with lap-joint, sides of top diagonally running multiple twill, body with twill diamonds, filled.

382. Covered basket, top with arrow twill, body weave twilled out of the weave.

383. Bag made of a folded banana leaf, Australia.

378

379

380

▽ 381

▽ 382

▽ 38

166

384

384, 385. *Tall thin bag of two palm leaves without stems, with fronds woven together. 384. Complete view. 385. Enlarged view of the bottom, height 400, length 270, width 140.*

386. *Box with high inverted lid, main part of the body a smooth weave, lid and lower body an unusual standing-out weave with special skein situation (twisting), Indonesia, height 180, length 160, width 160.*

387. *Left: bowl with rich weave (twisting of the palm-leaf straws). Right: cap with spiked palm-leave weave, likewise formed by a special skein situation. Left: height 140, diameter 190.*

388. *Basket, natural, compressed sack form, fine bamboo skeins, above wide, flat-lying zigzag twill, Japan.*

85   ▽ 387   387   386   ▽ 388

167

389. Sewing basket with latch and carrying ring, latch pieces made economically of the same material, noble basket-round shape, flat skeins, top rounds of wrapped spiral roll work.

390. Large sewing basket, basket-round, lid of flat skeins, body of pressed fitches with diamond pattern. Double hasps, many reinforcing fillets bound onto the stakes. Michelau work, height 220, length 350, width 254.

391. Large workbasket, willow skeins, flat-skein high-and-deep weave. Height 340, diameter 340.

392. Workbasket, white willow skeins, stakes carefully cut into each other, pressed fitches, complete evenness of the fitching strokes. Height 370, diameter 236.

393. Small sewing basket, of wide thin willow skeins, mild sheen of the growth layer (wax layer), simplest randing weave over and under one. Height 150, length 232, width 188.

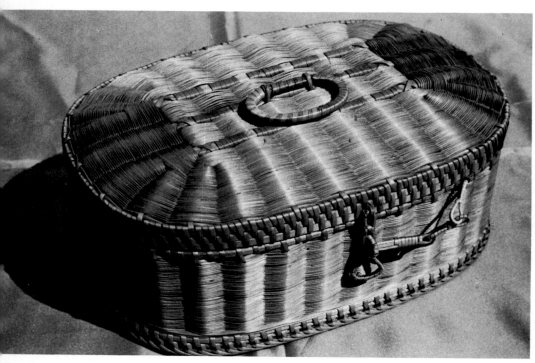

170

394. *Embroidery basket, white willow skeins (yellowed with age), latch and two handles, lightly flexible, completely of willow skeins, especially rich execution of the pressed fitches, circa 1850, Height 116, diameter 164.*

395. *Workbasket with circular top, white willow skeins, the simple latch livens up the full body.*

396. *Workbasket, willow skeins, high-and-deep weave, apple shape.*

397. *Workbasket, firm stand through inverted cone stump shape, lid falling into a notch, simple randing, rib effect of the stakes.*

398. *Large workbasket, rounded rectangle, willow skeins, alternating wide thick and narrow thin stakes, worked out with pressed fitches. Compare #251.*

399. *Sewing basket, willow skeins, high-and-deep weave.*

400. *Sewing basket, basket-round cylindrical form, simple randing. Lid falls onto a notch.*

401. Small sewing basket, willow skeins, waved, staved, unusual beginning of lid (center of bottom). Height 150, length 230, width 230. Compare #289.

402, 403. Small sewing basket with waved rim, willow skeins, flat skein bottom, lid attached, octagponal hoop form, circa 1880.Height 120, length 230, width 230.

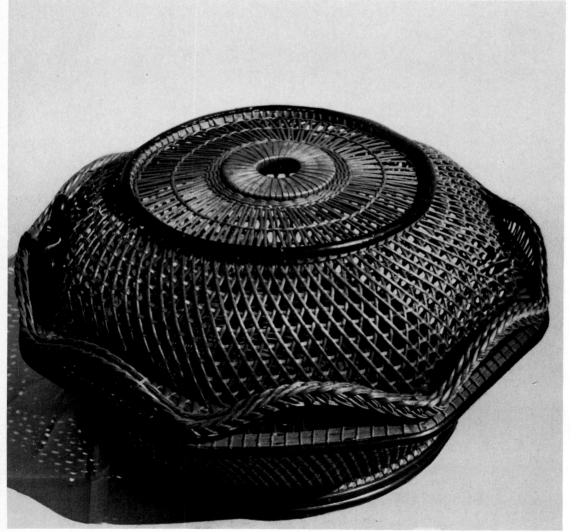

404. Mending basket, palm-leaf work, barrel shape, "thickly knitted". Height 330, diameter 306.

405. Small rush basket, fitched.

406. Handbag, palm-leaf work, next to it Japanese napkin rings, in front of that a peasant finger. Height 160, length 230, width 140.

407. Basket shop with old Upper Franconian smallest basket wares, from the Toy Museum, Nuremberg.

408. *Guitar-playing Indian, rush weave, Mexico.*

409. *Rider on horse, rush weave, height 430, length 420, width 140.*

410. *Pack mule, esparto grass, Spain, height 710, length 370, width 366.*

411. *Frog, straw braids wrapped over reed frame, height 240, length 420, width 240.*

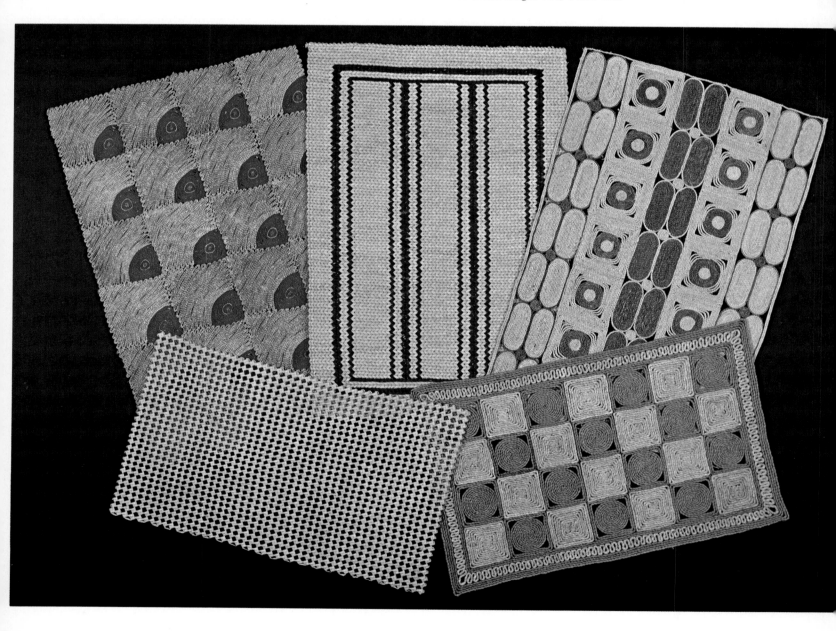

412. East Asian rugs, partly of maize leaves, lower left sieve weave of a table mat with special knotted weave. Large mats: length 900, width 600. Small: length 750, width 450.

413. Dollhouse armchair and baskets for child care, The Hague, Netherlands.

414. Dollhouse baskets, at right miniature Nuremberg egg baskets. Leather parts stamped. The Hague, Netherlands.

178

415. *Knitted fish, holding needles, wool or yarn, tied work of black lacquered reed and white whipcord, Old Michelau work, circa 1850, height 100, length 300.*

416. *Knitting barrel, willow skeins, with chain handle, height 144, diameter 96.*

417. *Duck-shaped knitting basket, willow skeins, black lacquered reed skeins as decoration, attachment hoops on the side.*

418. *Demountable wooden form for the duck (diminished!).*

419. *Knotted straw hat, decorated with light straw braid, carefully executed border, Alsace.*

420. *Small toy or holiday straw hat, knotted work, Isle of Ischia, circa 1970.*

421. *Small straw hat, sewn of straw braids, with woven cords.*

422. *Peasant hat, black straw braids, Lienz, Austria.*

423. *Top hat, willow skeins, randed, circa 1840.*

419

420

▽ 42

▽ 422   ▽ 423

424, 425. Knotted straw hat, rich decoration of straw braids, plaits and flowers of knotted straw.

426. Man's summer hat of fine white willow skeins, Old Michelau.

427. Knotted straw top hat, silk bands, Alsace.

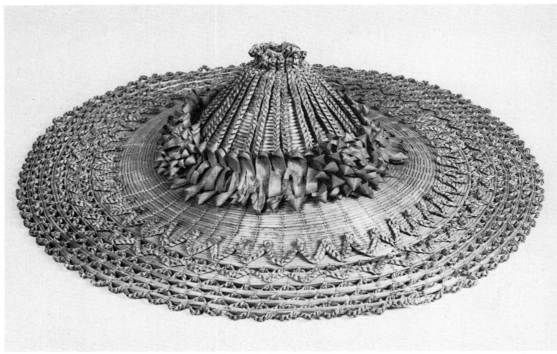

428

▽ 429

182

431. Children's sandals, uppers of woven leather straps.

432. Straw shoes, lined with cloth.

433. Sandals with binding straps.

434. Slippers, sewn of straw braids.

435. Slippers, woven of hard grass.

436. Cattail slippers, finely woven.

Addenda

Acknowledgements

The author would particularly like to thank the publishers for daring to present to the world, despite much work and expense, the generally unknown particulars of basket weaving. He thanks his successor, Director Ernst Schneider, for the negotiation of the book contract and for further assistance, above all for the preparation of numerous photographs of items from the Trade School collection, both antiques and present-day products of the school's creative activities.

In spite of the scope of the book, not all of the author's wishes could be fulfilled on account of the broad range of the contents, especially in regard to showing the works of outstanding basket manufacturers. The experienced old basket making firms and the handicraft workshops of Heinrich Murmann in Johannisthal, Kurt Schuetz in Selbersdorf, Kretz in Neuensorg and newer companies could be presented only briefly or not at all. Also, Gerd Backert and Waldemar Backert could, in the end, not be treated as the richness of their productivity and innovation deserved. The outstanding creations of the author's predecessor, Professor Daum, remained of necessity just as unmentioned as other fine works.

Translator's Note

I am the first to admit that I have no practical knowledge of basket making. I have tried to equate accepted German and English basket terminology, but at times I have not been able to find an English term by which to translate a German term, and have had to give a literal translation and hope the English-speaking reader will understand. The list of specialized terminology offers an extensive German-to-English glossary; the main index will provide a more inclusive English-to-German glossary.

In the text I have tried to write readable, understandable English without departing from the author's typically German sentence structure. The text could have been rewritten into smoother, simpler English, but I did not feel that I had the right to do so.   E.F.

Specialized Terminology

Aufbruch, aufbrechen: opening out; when the bottom is opened out, the bottom sticks are bent apart in ray form, without interruption, from the slath outward.

Aufbruchlage: opening-out area; after the slath, weaving goes on until the bottom sticks or stakes are divided evenly.

Auflage, aufgelegt: two-tone pairing; to make a colorful pattern for a part of a basket, a strand of another color is laid onto the stakes and woven in with them.

Aufrichter: spoke, upsetter; the standing stake, the stiffer willow that forms the framework of the basket.

Aufsteller: pricking up; the framework of the basket is bent upward before the upsetting.

Aufzug: raised decoration or strengthening applied as a wale, or as a plaited edging on a wrapped border.

Beistecken, Beisteckling: bye-staking, bye-stake: when the distance between the stakes is too great and the weave thereby too loose, one or more new stakes must be added between the original stakes.

Bindlage: slath; when the bottom cross is formed, from which the stakes are opened out, it must be made firm and bound together to form the slath.

Bodenholz: bottom sticks; the woven stakes that go into the weaving of the bottom star or base, for example, in a laundry basket.

Bodenkreuz: bottom cross; the bottom sticks or stakes which form the base or beginning, either laid loosely across each other or stuck into each other.

Breitenwechsel: varying width; use of weavers of different widths for the purpose of strengthening or of making a picturesque pattern.

Buenderlasarbeit: for decoration, brightening or strengthening, several willow stakes are laid flat against each other like leaves.

Dreigeflecht: triple weave; a slewed weave instead of the usual randing, with three weavers braided in horizontal spirals.

Dueten, Duetengeflecht: over stakes standing quite close together, wide thin weavers are woven into strong three-dimensional rounds that form, for example, small pyramids or braids.

Einkimmen: waling; the transitional weaving from base to body is made with three or four wales, because they form the shape and hold the stakes better. After that the randing, generally in single rounds, can begin.

Einschlag: 1. weft; the basket willows, the weavers that, in full willow work, are woven over the stakes to form the body and are placed tightly over each other; 2. the type of stake-woven borders that consist of more than a half stroke.

Fitze, fitzen: fitch, fitching: a strand of two willows, winding not only around the stakes like simple randing but also around each other.

Flechterische Mittel: weaving means; all technical processes that determine firmness, appearance and endurance in weaving work, for example, the number of strokes, length of stroke, weave direction, type and use of material, proportions, changes etc.

Flechtrichtung: weave direction; generally to the right, more rarely from right to left. In raising lapped borders the weave direction can run up, down, left, right or diagonally.

Gangweise Arbeit: through the repeating form of the willows, certain types of weaving are offered, above all in "struck work": layers, squares, slewing, "housing", in-and-out weaving.

Gehaengte Geflechte: hung weaves; the third type of weaving, defined according to the means of attachment. The hung weaves are like crocheted, knitted or hooked needlework. Every following row hangs onto the previous one.

Geschlagene Arbeit: fully or half- "struck" (stake-and-weaver) work; strands of full unsplit willows are beaten together after weaving, to make the weave firmer and thicker; this is done by hand or with a wooden or iron tool.

Geschnuerte Arbeit: bound work, old Michelau style; two sets of stakes, generally crossing at right angles, are bound together by cord. The horizontal, vertical or diagonal ties can be expanded into cross-stitched patterns.

Gestaebte Geflechte: staved weaves; they are staked weaves, usually held together or apart by horizontal fitches some distance apart.Frequently used in France.

Gestakte Geflechte: staked weaves; they always have the generally vertical strong, inflexible state of the stakes (spokes) and the thinner, softer state of the weavers: randed, layered, lapped and plaited weaves.

Gestochene Arbeit: "stuck", spaced work; old Upper Franconian-Michelau fine willow skein work. The spiral full willow weft, later round rattan, is held together, usually at a distance, by willow rods or palm-leaf blades with lapping and binding strokes.

Gezogene Arbeit: "drawn work" (of stakes only); of willow tops, round rattan, bamboo rods etc. a. Fully drawn work: the willows are drawn in together at wide intervals, plaited in circular form at first, so that they go outward and wind their way back in a bow to the middle of the bowl. To give form to the originally flat, even weave, the strands or stakes, mostly of more than one rod, are drawn in toward the middle of the basket. Through the manner of drawing them in, the intended hollow form of the basin or bowl is formed. b. Half-drawn work: a typical base of stakes, divided and closed off by waling, is stuck with thin, flexible willow tops. These are then woven under in bows, as in fully drawn work.

Haeuseln: "housing"; basket bodies etc. formed of full willows are bound between every two stakes, in rows or at intervals, with figure-eight strokes. Between the individual "little houses", that is, squares, one stake interval always remains free.

Halbschlag: half-stroke; the weaver goes over (or under) one or more stakes, and then under (or over) the next one.

Handspan: hand splint; one or more annular rings of suitable tree wood, taken off by hand, rigid or flexible, to the thinness of paper.

Hoch- und Tiefgeflecht: high and deep weave; two layers of strong, not windable stakes are laid over each other at right angles without attachment. The stakes form the vertical portion, the rigid rounds the horizontal. Both are bound by the third horizontal, thin winding weavers.

Kimme: wale; a fitching procedure, but with three or more weavers.

Kipprand: rolled border; a border woven of stakes, with only half-strokes.

Koeper, Koeperschlag: twill, twill stroke; an expression taken from textile weaving. Simple in-and-out strokes, but running over or under one, two or more stakes.

Korbholz: basket wood; weavers for the body of the basket.

Mehrweidigkeit: multiple weaves; two or more weavers, splints, skeins etc., that run unbroken, right next to each other, through the entire weave.

Rippe: rib; a firm, not very flexible willow rod, especially as used in splinted bowls, Hessian baskets etc.

Rueckschritt: "back step"; reaching back to a previous stake in closing stake borders, around one stake. Also in plaited borders.

Ruecksprung: "back jump"; reaching back around two or more previous stakes lying to the left in closing and plaiting.

Rumpfholz: body wood; basket wood, the softer willows for weaving into, "working out" of the body stakes.

Schicht, schichten, Schichtschlag: layer, layering, layer stroke; the unique form of the repeating willow rod requires its own ways of weaving. The nature of the layer is that at the beginning of the body weaving a layer willow is inserted between every two stakes. Thereby the layer strokes run somewhat diagonally upwards to the right.

Schilderhaeuser: "sentry boxes"; corners standing out of the flat woven area, where wide and stiff skeins or splints are woven into strongly arched basket shapes. Through deliberate and controlled exaggeration of this "unwanted error" there arise lively three-dimensional weaving patterns, particularly in construction weaving.

Schlag: stroke; in weaving it means a single, repeated weaving procedure annd attachment. A stroke goes over one or more stakes, under one or more, outside again in constant repetition. It can also begin with binding under.

Schlaglaenge: stroke length; it is not a measure of length, but the number of over- or underbound stakes. The metrical length is determined only by the thickness and interval of the stakes ansd by their number.

Spaltlage: needles and threads; split willows, slit open in the middle (needles), used in the base cross. (The "threads" are inserted through the slits.)

Speiche: spoke; the strong ribs, stakes, upsetters, especially in splint weaving, called "Schbacha" in Bavarian-Franconian dialect.

Stake: stake; strong stiff willow or rod, of which the skeletal ribs of the body are formed.

Stakenraender, stakenverflechtende Raender: stake borders, stakewoven borders; the stakes coming out of the body weave are plaited toward each other in a multitude of ways: rolled, trac, plain or plaited borders.

Spalter, Weidenspalter: cleaver, willow cleaver; a round, fairly wedge-shaped tool of hard wood, bone, metal etc. Also called a slitter, ripper, separator etc.

Ueber- und Unterbindung: over- and underbinding; an expression taken from textile weaving. (It refers to fastening the beginning or end of a weaver over or under a stake.)

Versetzung, Versetzungszahl: change of stroke, changing number; in twill weaving, also in forming cubes, every following round of the longer strokes must be displaced to the right or left.

Versetzungsrichtung: changing direction; for the more picturesque body designs such as zigzag, herringbone, lightning strokes and other twills, for diamonds or other rectangular figures, the direction of change must go first to the right and then back to the left.

Viergeflecht: four-ply weave; a staked weave with four skeins or willows with a horizontal axis of symmetry, as opposed to triple weave.

Vorschritt: "forward step"; in the border, reaching to the next stake to the right, thus one stake.

Vorsprung: "forward jump", in the border, generally over two or more stakes; the second spoke ahead is reached and laid onto.

Zaeunen: randing; the rounds of simple weaving, especially used in Upper Franconia for the simplest in-and-out type of weaving around the stakes.

Select Bibliography

Bomann, W., Baeuerliches Hauswesen und Tagewerk im alten Niedersachsen, Weimar 1933.

Brueckner, Georg, Die Koerbe des Meininger Landes, 1852.

Gagel, Georg, Korbwarenkatalog um 1839, Michelau /Coburg.

Gandert, August, Tragkoerbe in Hessen, Kassel 1963.

Haevernick, Walter, Die Formen des Tragkorbes in Thueringen, in Beitraege zur deutschen Volks- und Altertumskunde, Hamburg 1954.

Kunz, Heinrich, Peddigrohrflechten, Bern 1959.

Lehmann, Johannes, Systematik der Geflechte, Leipzig, no year.

Moser, Oskar, Vom geflochtenen Kasten, Carinthia I, Vol. 133, Klagenfurt 1943.

Schier, Bruno, Das Flechten im Lichte der historischen Volkskunde, Frankfurt am Main 1951.

Wilckens, v. Leonie, Das Puppenhaus, Munich 1978.

Will, Christoph, Kleines allgemeines Lehrbuch der Korbflechterei, Bamberg, no year.

Will, Christoph, Peddigrohrflechten, Ravensburg.

Will, Christoph, Weidenschienenflechten, Ravensburg.

Wright, Dorothy, Baskets and Basketry, Newton Abbot /Devon 1959.

PERIODICALS

"Das Flechtwerk", trade paper, about 20 yearly volumes since 1949, Verlag Patschke, Neustadt bei Coburg, no longer in print. Some issues still available at the Basket Museum, Michelau.

"Der Korbflechterlehrling", addendum to "Flechtwerk".

"Der Korbweidenanbau", addendum to "Flechtwerk".

The articles in the periodicals named are mainly by the author.

Existing in manuscript form at the School for Basket Weaving:

1. Bibliography of Basket Weaving, by C. R. Arntzeniuns, 1956; School for Basket Weaving, Lichtenfels.
2. Bibliography of Basket Weaving, made under the direction of E. Schneider at the School for Basket Weaving, Lichtenfels.
3. Ongoing reports of the German Basket Museum, existing in great numbers, by the author. The collection is being continued and, if time permits, will be expanded.
4. Memoranda of the School for Basket Weaving, Lichtenfels, on various subjects. By the author and the faculty.
5. Ongoing scientific reports of the School for Basket Weaving, Lichtenfels, commissioned by the Bavarian Economic Ministry, by the author and faculty of the school, with illustrations.

Creation and Production of Pictured Objects

List of Workshops, Museums and Collections

Index of Pictures

Index

The numbers in bold face refer to the illustrations.

Middle Ages, weaving in the, 14
Milan, Italy, 59
Mitwitz, Germany, 31, 48, **35, 294**
Model, 36
Model chair, **179-180**
Money box, Thuringian, **360**
Mons-Ziggler, 68
Muelhausen, Alsace, Museum, **425**
Munich, Bavarian National Museum, 15, 71

Naila, State Trade School for Embroidery, **176**
Name, false, 31
Napkin rings, Japanese, **406**
Naples, National Museum, 14
Natural coloring, 53
Natural weaving material, 9
Natural reed, 10, 26
Natural reed skein, **140**
Near East, 60
Needles and Threads, 39, 42
Nepal, 60
Netherlands, The, 14, 24-25, 58, 70
Neumann, Balthasar, 8
Neusiedler See, Austria, 64
Nitrolacquer, 11
North Africa, 10, 12, 60
North America, 60
North Germany, 25, **157**
Norway, 49
Nubbin foot, 41
Numbers, application of, 42, 48
Nuremberg, Germany, 58, 67, **149, 241, 244**
Nuremberg Economic Institute, 67
Nuremberg egg basket, 53-54, 70, **258-259, 261**
Nuremberg, Germanic National Museum, 15, 57, 71
Nuremberg, State Commercial Institute, 71
Nuremberg, Toy Museum, 15, **407**
Nut bowl, **364**
Nut tree, 23
Nut tree hand splint, **261**

Oak, 23, 30
Octagonal weave, 36-37, 48-49, **27, 31, 183-184**
Offenbach, Leather Museum, 70
Organization of the Basket Industry, 68
Original numbers, 42
Original weave, 47
Orlishausen, Friedrich, of Lichtenfels, 33
Ornament, Moorish, 10
Ornament, old Cretan, **4**
Ornament, running dog, 14, 51
Ornamental Geometry of the Greeks, 14
Ornamentation, early Germanic, 13
Ornamentation, woven, 13, 50
Ornamenting, 50
Oseberg Ship, 59
Ostwald, Wilhelm, 42, 50

Pack mule of esparto grass, **410**
Painting, 53
Palatinate area, Germany, 30, 57
Palm basket, Mitwitz (working drawing), **35**
Palm leaf, 11, 25, 30, 39, **211, 384-385, 387**
Palm leaf, Cuban, 31, 52, 63, **66-67**
Palm-leaf spiral work, **294**
Palm-leaf stroke, **118**
Palm-leaf work, 25, 34, 40, 47, 59, **357, 406**
Palm-leaf work, Indonesian, 48, **38**
Palm reed, 25, 30-31, 60, **69, 188, 190**
Panama hat, 64
Panel weave, **147, 149**
Panel weaver, 7
Pappenheim, Germany, 57

Partition, 42, **361**
Peasant finger, 11, **406**
Pegging, 42
Peeled veneer, 23
Peeled veneer splint, 44
Philippines, 30, **115, 173-174**
Picking, 39
Pine, 10, 23
Pine fine splint, **58**
Pine hand splint, 11, **13, 80, 210, 212, 308**
Pine ribs, **254**
Pine, Scotch, 20, 23
Pine splint, 11, **91, 351**
Pine splint, hand-drawn, 10
Pine splint wrapping, **333**
Planing bench, 34
Planing machine, 23
Plant ornaments, Greek, **328**
Plastic foil, **137**
Plastic ribbon, **226**
Plastic skein, **136**
Platter, **310-318**
Play pen, 11
Plexiglas, **138**
Ploen, Germany, 24
Pointed foot, 41
Poland, 24, 59, 64
Pole rattan, 30-31, **356**
Polyethylene, 10, 24
Polynesia, 61
Pond reed, 63-64
Pond rush, 63
Poplar, 23, 44
Portugal, 52, 59
Potato basket, 36, 41
Pottery, 12
Pre-Columbian Era, 12
Pretzel, 11
Pretzel knot, 40
Prischmann, Otto, of Leipzig, 71
Privet, 22
Processional palm, 59
Profile plane, 62
Protective construction, 12
Provision basket, **308**
Puppert, Johann, 15, **194**
Puppert, Master, 70
Puppertla basket, 54, **194**
Pussy willow, 31
Pyrogallic acid, 52

Quartering, **361**

Radial splint, **158-159**
Raffia bast, 31
Rander, 11
Randing, 37, 39, 50, 52
Randing, simple, 38, 49
Randing skein, 62, **93, 259**
Randing weave, 50, **4**
Rapping, 9
Rapping iron, 32, 36, **94**
Rapport, 43, **127**
Rattan, 9-10, 23, 25-26, 29, 34, 44, 57-58, 60, 64, **70, 72**
Rattan armchair, **185-187**
Rattan band, 30-31, **133-135, 356**
Rattan machine, 35
Rattan reed, 31, **182**
Rattan skein, 30-31, **133, 135**
Rattan splint, **118**
Rattan types, 29
Rattan weaving, 31, 70
Rear legs, forked, **257**

Red or blue band rattan, 31
Reed, 9, 11-12, 23, 25, 59, **72, 85**
Reed bast, 26, 31
Reed ribbon, 10
Reed, Spanish, 21, 31
Reed work, 63
Reemtsma, Albin, 35
Rehau Plastic, 24
Reidt, Professor, 70
Rhine river, 69
Rhoen, 8, 57, **239, 251**
Ribbon, 21
Ribbon rattan, 21, 31, **210**
Ribbon reed, 29
Rib, **87-88**
Rib, randed, **160**
Richter, Ludwig, **3**
Rider on horseback, **409**
Ring bundle, 36
Ring fence, 36, **146, 154, 156**
Ripstraw, 30
Ritz, Dr. Josef Maria, 71
Rock tomb, 12
Rococo armchair, **183**
Rod, 20-21
Rod skein, 23
Roll, 21
Roll inlay, 25
Rolled border, 41, **119-121**
Roman, 15, 38, 62
Root splint, 23
Roper's belt, **232, 235-236**
Rosenthal, Philipp, Porcelain Factory, **177**
Rotterdam, The Netherlands, 26
Round plane, 62
Round rattan, 30, 40, **104, 141, 181, 227, 270, 289, 307, 357**
Round rattan ribbon, 23
Round rattan splitting, **109**
Round rattan work, **104**
Rounds, lightly drawn-out, **8**
Rucksack, 59
Rudnik, Poland, 59
Rug, 60, 63, **412**
Rug beater, 26, 64
Rumania, 24, 39, 59
Running dog (see also meander), 14, 51-52
Rush, 9, 11, 24, 39, 51-52, 59, 63
Rush basket, fitched, **405**
Rush chair, Worpswede, **178**
Rush figure, 64
Rush string, 25
Rush tube, straw, 8
Rush weave, **408-409**
Rush weaving, 24, **36**
Rush work, 14, 63
Russia, 59
Rye, 25
Rye straw, 58

Sack form, compressed, **388**
Saleen (synthetic material), 10, 24
Sallow, 21, 34, **108**
Salt-water rush, 9
Sandal, 59, **428-436**
Sandal, child's, **431**
Sandal, old Egyptian, **428**
Sardinia, 21, 24, 30, 51, 59, 61, **55, 68, 220-221, 344**
Sardinian fisherman, **85, 220**
"Sausage border", 41
Scandinavia, 59
Schoenau vor dem Walde, East Germany, 15
Schongauer, Martin, **5**